Human Resource Management: A Very Short Introduction

VERY SHORT INTRODUCTIONS are for anyone wanting a stimulating and accessible way into a new subject. They are written by experts, and have been translated into more than 45 different languages.

The series began in 1995, and now covers a wide variety of topics in every discipline. The VSI library currently contains over 700 volumes—a Very Short Introduction to everything from Psychology and Philosophy of Science to American History and Relativity—and continues to grow in every subject area.

Very Short Introductions available now:

ABOLITIONISM Richard S. Newman
THE ABRAHAMIC RELIGIONS
    Charles L. Cohen
ACCOUNTING Christopher Nobes
ADOLESCENCE Peter K. Smith
ADVERTISING Winston Fletcher
AERIAL WARFARE Frank Ledwidge
AESTHETICS Bence Nanay
AFRICAN AMERICAN RELIGION
    Eddie S. Glaude Jr
AFRICAN HISTORY John Parker and
    Richard Rathbone
AFRICAN POLITICS Ian Taylor
AFRICAN RELIGIONS
    Jacob K. Olupona
AGEING Nancy A. Pachana
AGNOSTICISM Robin Le Poidevin
AGRICULTURE Paul Brassley and
    Richard Soffe
ALEXANDER THE GREAT
    Hugh Bowden
ALGEBRA Peter M. Higgins
AMERICAN BUSINESS HISTORY
    Walter A. Friedman
AMERICAN CULTURAL HISTORY
    Eric Avila
AMERICAN FOREIGN RELATIONS
    Andrew Preston
AMERICAN HISTORY Paul S. Boyer
AMERICAN IMMIGRATION
    David A. Gerber
AMERICAN INTELLECTUAL
    HISTORY
    Jennifer Ratner-Rosenhagen

AMERICAN LEGAL HISTORY
    G. Edward White
AMERICAN MILITARY HISTORY
    Joseph T. Glatthaar
AMERICAN NAVAL HISTORY
    Craig L. Symonds
AMERICAN POETRY David Caplan
AMERICAN POLITICAL HISTORY
    Donald Critchlow
AMERICAN POLITICAL PARTIES
    AND ELECTIONS L. Sandy Maisel
AMERICAN POLITICS
    Richard M. Valelly
THE AMERICAN PRESIDENCY
    Charles O. Jones
THE AMERICAN REVOLUTION
    Robert J. Allison
AMERICAN SLAVERY
    Heather Andrea Williams
THE AMERICAN SOUTH
    Charles Reagan Wilson
THE AMERICAN WEST Stephen Aron
AMERICAN WOMEN'S HISTORY
    Susan Ware
AMPHIBIANS T. S. Kemp
ANAESTHESIA Aidan O'Donnell
ANALYTIC PHILOSOPHY
    Michael Beaney
ANARCHISM Colin Ward
ANCIENT ASSYRIA Karen Radner
ANCIENT EGYPT Ian Shaw
ANCIENT EGYPTIAN ART AND
    ARCHITECTURE Christina Riggs
ANCIENT GREECE Paul Cartledge

For more information visit our website

www.oup.com/vsi/

Adrian Wilkinson

HUMAN RESOURCE MANAGEMENT

A Very Short Introduction

OXFORD
UNIVERSITY PRESS

OXFORD
UNIVERSITY PRESS

Great Clarendon Street, Oxford, OX2 6DP,
United Kingdom

Oxford University Press is a department of the University of Oxford.
It furthers the University's objective of excellence in research, scholarship,
and education by publishing worldwide. Oxford is a registered trade mark of
Oxford University Press in the UK and in certain other countries

© Adrian Wilkinson 2022

The moral rights of the author have been asserted

First edition published in 2022

Impression: 1

All rights reserved. No part of this publication may be reproduced, stored in
a retrieval system, or transmitted, in any form or by any means, without the
prior permission in writing of Oxford University Press, or as expressly permitted
by law, by licence or under terms agreed with the appropriate reprographics
rights organization. Enquiries concerning reproduction outside the scope of the
above should be sent to the Rights Department, Oxford University Press, at the
address above

You must not circulate this work in any other form
and you must impose this same condition on any acquirer

Published in the United States of America by Oxford University Press
198 Madison Avenue, New York, NY 10016, United States of America

British Library Cataloguing in Publication Data
Data available

Library of Congress Control Number: 2021948455

ISBN 978-0-19-871473-6

Printed in Great Britain by
Ashford Colour Press Ltd, Gosport, Hampshire

Links to third party websites are provided by Oxford in good faith and
for information only. Oxford disclaims any responsibility for the materials
contained in any third party website referenced in this work.

To Erin and Aidan

Contents

Acknowledgements

My thanks to Tony Dundon, Stewart Johnstone, Chantal Gallant, Brad Bowden, and Alison Howson for their input.

Thanks to Erin Wilkinson for providing research support. Thanks also to Aidan Wilkinson and Joanne Dolley who kindly read drafts and provided feedback.

At OUP I would like to thank Jenny Nugee, Matthew Cotton, Luciana O'Flaherty, and Christina Fleischer.

List of illustrations

List of tables

Chapter 1
What is Human Resource Management and why does it matter?

While there is no universally accepted definition of Human Resource Management (HRM), in simple terms, it is about the relationship between employer and employee and how this is managed. It covers all aspects of how people are managed, including working conditions and how decisions about work are made when we go to work for someone, or we employ someone to work for us. It is worth noting that the average employee will spend 80,000 hours of his or her life at work. That equates to more time than we are likely to spend on any other activity during our lifetimes. We spend more time with our work colleagues than many of us spend with our families. The management of our working lives is therefore a topic that affects nearly all of us and has important ramifications for society as a whole. Recent work by Bryson and MacKerron found that paid work is ranked lower than 39 other common activities people engage in, except for being sick in bed (Table 1). Well-being at work varies depending on where you work (at home, in an office, or elsewhere); whether you combine work with other activities; whether you work with others; when you work; and your personal and household characteristics. Some of this can be influenced by the choices we make for ourselves and the decisions made for us by others (managers) as well as public policy that governs the working environment. If we are not as individuals complete masters of our destiny, we do have choices as a society.

Table 1. Bryson and MacKerron's ranking of common activities

Intimacy, making love
Theatre, dance
Sports, exercising
Singing, performing
Chatting, socializing
Walking, hiking
Hunting, fishing
Drinking alcohol
Hobbies, arts
Meditating, religious activities
Sporting event
Childcare
Pet care
Listening to music
Games, puzzles
Shopping, errands
Gambling, betting
Computer games
Eating, snacking
Cooking, preparing food
Drinking tea/coffee
Reading
Listening to speech/podcast
Washing, dressing, grooming
Sleeping, resting, relaxing
Smoking
Browsing the internet
Text, email, social media
Housework, DIY

Travelling, commuting
Meeting, seminar, class
Admin, finance, organizing
Waiting, queuing
Care or help for adults
Working, studying
Sick in bed

Human Resource Management (HRM) is about the management of people in the context of an employment relationship. In short, if we are working for someone and getting paid (compensated) we are in an employment relationship. For some work is a daily grind, but not everyone views work in a negative sense. People can enjoy the work itself, or they might enjoy the contribution they can make. They might enjoy being part of a community in the workplace. People who win the lottery, for instance, will often continue to work when they have no need of the pay cheque.

There are no simple scientific laws (although there are employment laws) to apply in HRM, and much therefore depends on context. However, people differ, not only from each other but in their attitudes and reactions from one day to the next. This is what makes HRM a source of both fascination and frustration. The term 'herding cats' comes to mind. Thus, it is hard to make predictions in the same way as you can in, say, physics. Managing people in a large manufacturing firm is different from running a corner store. Working at a merchant bank is different from working on the docks or at a hospital. Equally, how HRM is managed will vary across cultures and countries. The USA is rather more individualistic than, say, mainland Europe, where things tend to be viewed in more social and collectivist terms. Equally, in Japan, age, family, and respect for honour are central. This has implications for HRM. If there is a view that individual motivation and capability is the key to success, practices may well be configured to facilitate this. If there is more emphasis on collective routes to achieve tasks then again practices may be configured to allow for that. Legislative and other forms of regulation vary considerably across countries, as do institutional arrangements (law, rules, custom, and practice). In the USA, a 'hire-and fire-at-will' philosophy means staff can be treated differently from those in, for example, Germany where laws and regulations mean making workers redundant or dismissing them for other reasons is a slower and more considered process. Here we can see the ingredients for misunderstandings when multinational corporations take their assumptions and institutions to another part of the world on the basis of best practice. Differing institutional contexts also help explain variation in the prevalence of zero hours contracts or the conditions of the gig economy.

When did HRM begin? The industrial revolution was the crucible for the creation of modern management. With the steam engine as the driver, new modes of thought accompanied the industrial revolution. Indeed, if we were to look to the most revolutionary change that drove the industrial revolution it is a transformation in transport. First associated with Britain's canal systems, then steamships and trains, ease of transport allowed for a concentration of people and resources while, at the same time, exposing previously sheltered industries to competition and innovation. As there were no business schools or colleges given over to the training of managers, most firms initially recruited managers internally, either through the delegation of family members or by promoting workers from the shop floor. Firms slowly realized, however, that although technical knowledge was a useful attribute in running a business it was not as important as general managerial ability: a capacity to identify operational problems, recruit and motivate staff, match supply with demand, and keep an eye on the innovations implemented by competitors. The British historian Sydney Pollard notes that Britain's coal industry was the largest supplier of managers to Britain's expanding factories and mills. Not only was this industry the first to use steam power with the introduction of the Newcomen engine (the world's first atmospheric steam engine), in 1712, the workforces were also far larger than those found elsewhere, the typical coal mine employing hundreds of workers at a time when most workshops engaged a handful.

Organizations grew simply too large to be properly controlled by their owners, so managers became responsible for the organization. That is not to say everything was new. It has been pointed out that good parts of the management armoury were available prior to the industrial revolution, given most organizations have to deal with issues of coordination and control. And the functions, ideologies, practices, and theories of management have changed over time since the foundation of modern management. But the concepts and applications of management have now become so pervasive in our society that they are prevalent not only in for-profit firms but also in non-profits, cooperatives, state agencies, and any aspect of society that requires organization.

Although people worked in pre-industrial times, it was the industrial revolution that led to greater formalization and the creation of a factory regime. This created manager and worker relationships, with the employer providing tools and equipment and paying for work. Such pay was used to obtain the things workers needed to live (food, shelter, etc.) rather than them working the land on which they lived. Equally, their previous relationship with landowners, which was more personal (which is not to say it was not exploitative), was replaced by more impersonal relations between employer and employee, with supervisors who were not owners but the beginning of a professional cadre who later became management. The supervisor hired and fired as well as organized and instructed work.

With the first factories (the 'dark satanic mills' described by the English poet William Blake) came systems. As production moved to a larger scale, masters built factories and installed machinery to take advantage of market and technological opportunities. They also needed a new sort of labour, one that was more disciplined and literate than those of the pre-industrial order. It made little difference when individual workers started work when each operated their own hand tools, however when mechanized production was introduced it required all to work to the same exact schedule. Initially, mechanization was solely restricted to the spinning of cotton and, to a lesser degree, wool. With increased competition, the employers also brought hand-weavers into the mills and sought to improve the quality of production through increased supervision. Although the early factories did employ large number of children sourced from orphanages and poorhouses, this proved a brief stage in the production process as—with higher levels of capitalization—employers sought higher productivity through literate and more skilled workforces and children were inefficient and hard to train. This coincided with laws forbidding child labour driven by humanitarian concerns and by 1851 most children no longer worked in factories.

As productivity soared, wholesale and retail prices collapsed. By 1860, a metre of cloth could be purchased for 13 per cent of its 1790 price. Not only did this make clothing far cheaper, it also forced constant innovation to compensate for falling prices. The factory owners also needed to think in a rather different and more systematic way in terms of recruiting and rewarding workers. But factories in these times were not how we would recognize them today, at least not in western industrialized countries. They were messy, noisy, chaotic, and dangerous. The factory regime created enormous social problems both in and outside the factory, and living conditions were dismal. So, the labour problem had a knock-on effect and created broader social problems. In Elizabeth Gaskell's novel *North and South*, set in the fictional industrial town of Milton (Manchester), we see the heroine witness grim working (and living) conditions. The factory clock governed life (after all, time is now seen as money) rather than the seasons or the weather, moulding the culture of capitalism. Indeed, the economic historian David Landes argued that timepieces even more than the steamship drove the economic development of the West as factory owners gave watches to punctual workers and workers brought their own timepieces to work so they did not need to trust the factory clock. This explains the tradition in some cultures of being given a watch upon retirement as your time was now your own....

In all this we see the emerging roots of HRM. The early campaigns for worker welfare in the 18th and 19th centuries were driven by a mix of humanitarian, religious, philanthropic, and business motives. Work began to be regulated with restrictions on children working in factories and then on working hours. Some employers took innovative approaches such as Robert Owen (the Welsh philanthropist and social reformer) who established New Lanark (near Glasgow), a spinning mill village with housing for workers and schools for children based on paternalistic principles and setting out a goal of an eight-hour workday with the slogan, 'eight hours labour, eight hours recreation, eight hours rest'. The Cadbury family (Quaker industrialists) built Bournville village (just outside Birmingham) in the 1890s to locate their cocoa and chocolate factory for their workers, who were provided with good wages and working conditions. Cadbury's also introduced works committees and pensions as well as making provision for parks and medical services. Organizations increasingly began to offer workplace amenities such as medical care, housing, and libraries. At the same time, functionaries and departments specializing in HR processes such as hiring, payroll, and record-keeping emerged.

But if we can detect the growing shoots of management in earlier times, most people see Frederick Winslow Taylor (an American engineer and consultant) as the founder of modern management in the early 20th century. Taylor developed the idea of 'scientific management' and argued that efficiency in business could be achieved through observing scientific principles and close monitoring. Science was to be applied to a 'fair day's work'. Managers took responsibility by replacing rule of thumb systems of craft workers and reduced these to rules, laws, and formulas allowing for less skilled workers to replace craft workers. Managers would instruct workers on what to do, how to do it, and how much time to take to do it. In short, managers did the thinking and workers carried out the orders. Henry Ford, the American industrialist, adopted these principles in the context of mass production and assembly lines to build cars. The system did run into problems of motivation and morale. A huge machine works at Pittsburgh in the USA in 1906 needed to hire 12,000 men and women to fill 10,000 jobs as they needed to factor in the haemorrhaging of staff. Years later, this was also the experience in Italian car factories, with many more people employed than could work there if they all turned up. The tyranny of machines and the factory system governing the lives of workers featured in Charlie Chaplin's famous film *Modern Times*, which satirizes the factory process as developed by Henry Ford, in the 1920s, with his factory worker running around trying to tighten screws wherever he went, failing to keep up and eventually being sucked into the machine (Figure 1).

While Taylor tended to ignore the human factor in efficiency, the newly emerging discipline of personnel management embraced it. The same period saw a shift from direct systems of management (personal supervision, traditional paternalism, and simple piecework systems) to more complex technical systems of management and bureaucratic forms of employment. The Human Relations School sought to put workers more into the foreground of management systems and to see them as not just necessary cogs in the machinery of work, but as people with broader needs and interests. HRM pioneers drawing from writers like Mary Follett (an American thinker and political philosopher) at the turn of the 20th century began to lay out the principles of modern personnel

1. Charlie Chaplin in *Modern Times*.

methods with progressive changes in management style so as to humanize the workplace.

A bigger impetus to HRM was provided by the First World War, which increased the need for complex systems to recruit, train, and reward large numbers of workers. As organizations became larger and more complex, so HRM comes to the fore. We should note that the term HRM is used in different and confusing ways. It can mean three different things. First, it is an overall term to refer to managing people in organizations. In this sense HRM is found wherever there is employment. Second, it is also used with regard to the specific function: the HRM department. Third, in the academic literature it often refers to a 'new model' approach to people management dating from the 1990s and the 'discovery' of people as a strategic resource.

The professional HRM function has often been criticized as fulfilling a large administrative function rather than contributing to strategic goals directly as 'management' itself. All large organizations have HRM departments often with specialists within them responsible for dealing with recruitment, selection, training, talent management, performance management, reward, and employment relations. In smaller firms these roles are often taken by one of the senior managers, but once the numbers rise and it becomes difficult to deal with people on an individual basis an HRM function is usually established. In large multinational organizations the function may be dealing with employees across the globe with all the complexity that entails.

Traditionally the HRM function was seen as much more about dealing with staffing problems rather than workforce optimization. This was the backdrop for the rise of the 'new model' HRM, in the mid-1980s, a model that promised to develop and utilize the potential of human resources in pursuit of the organization's strategic objectives, a promise that informed the work of management researchers and excited practitioners.

Today, in an era of globalization, several factors have emerged that heighten the significance and complexity of HRM, including global sourcing, regional trade agreements, and labour standards, as well as cultural differences and innovation driven by competition. As traditional sources of competitive advantage evaporate such as access to capital, protected markets, and proprietary technologies, firms are looking to how they manage employees to provide a competitive edge. This includes managing and improving skills, capabilities, and behaviours. In fact, the harsh reality is that people are more often seen as a cost to be minimized, particularly in tough times. Senior managers have more often tried to minimize the impact of employees on performance by substituting capital for labour where possible (i.e. investing in technology and automating work, which reduces the need for staff) and designing bureaucratic organizations that place an emphasis on rule-following rather than facilitating initiative and empowerment.

It is fair to say that HRM rhetoric ('people are our most important asset'), while often espoused by organizations, has often been regarded cynically at the employee level. The practice of HRM is often accorded low status in organizational strategies, and the traditional separation of those who manage from those who actually do the work persists, contrary to the HRM ideal of workers being empowered and using their talents. Workers are also sceptical as they note the difference between their experience and the rhetoric.

Nevertheless, we have seen something of a revolution taking place in many organizations today. Managers, whether they explicitly acknowledge a human resource focus or not, are now actively interested in getting staff more motivated, engaged, and committed so as to meet demands and deliver organizational returns. This has been especially true of the service sector, the growth of which has come parallel to the growth of HRM. HRM has been embraced as transformative in this domain, where, from the perspective of customers, workers are the product (more than in manufacturing and design firms, where creativity in pursuit of product and systems innovations and efficiencies are seen as critical).

Whether in the 'laboratory' of university HRM departments or in the gritty reality of the factory floor, there is no single model of HRM to be applied. Indeed, the discipline has stretched to accommodate horizons beyond the traditional Taylorist focal point of large-scale manufacturing. The subject of HRM covers the small owner-managed textile sweatshops in Brick Lane, London, as well as the high-tech behemoths such as Apple, Facebook, and Google of Silicon Valley in California. Thus HRM covers individual and collective relations, the whole range of HR practices and processes, line management activities, as well as those of HR specialists, and both managerial and non-managerial actors.

The history and evolution of HRM emphasizes its long-standing concern with a **human** focus on employee well-being. As noted, this focus was much in evidence in early developments in the areas of occupational health and safety in the 19th century but we now see this focus reflected in issues such as equality and diversity and work–life balance. At its root, HRM focuses on managing employment relationships, as well as the implicit and explicit agreements established between individuals and organizations. How one balances the needs and interests of employees against the needs and interests of the organization is a hard path to navigate. The tensions between different models of HRM's role in firms, such as that between an 'employee champion' and a 'business partner' role in the organization, have been the subject of much debate in the literature. In the 1950s the Austrian management educator Peter Drucker joked that personnel management was about all those things that do not deal with the work of people and that are not management. More than half a century later, we can say that things have moved on, and what Drucker regarded as having been neglected—the organization of work and the organization of people to do the work—is front and centre.

HRM also focuses on employees as a **resource** in delivering performance. Much of the recent interest in HRM is about individual practices, or combinations, so-called bundles that promise enhanced productivity. HRM focuses on individual practices that ensure employee ability and motivation to perform effectively, such as: recruitment and selection to ensure that the best and the brightest talent is brought into the organization to fulfil its needs; training and development to develop staff skills; performance appraisal to assess performance and identify developmental requirements; and the management of performance and rewards. Talent Management became the mantra of recent years, although there are dangers if it becomes focused on a select few, creating a divisive and demotivating effect on the many, carrying a message that others lack talent and by implication contribute little.

While much of the literature on HRM has focused on the needs and concerns of employees in organizations (as well as their potential value as resources contributing to organizational performance), there is also a focus on **management**, including the changing role of the HR function, its organization, and professionalization as the HR function moves away from administrative and transactional requirements of personnel matters, towards taking a more strategic role focusing on managing change and building organizational culture.

The employment relationship has psychological, legal, economic, and political aspects, and an employment exchange involves ongoing negotiation between unequal parties. Keith Sisson, an employment relations professor, sees this as being about the institutions involved in governing the employment relationship, the people and organizations that make and administer them, and the rule-making involved, as well as the outcomes. Institutions include laws, customs, and practice, as well as the substantive rules that cover the 'what' of the employment relationship and procedural rules that deal with the 'how'. As Sisson observes, managers make rules and employees are expected to follow them.

Employment law is part of our story, and indeed the contract of employment lays out the rights and responsibilities of employers and employees. At its simplest, employees receive wages in return for which employers acquire the right to direct them, but of course the contract is seen in law as being between equal parties, which is a fiction. Whereas actors and professional footballers may sit down to negotiate a contract (or their lawyers do this on their behalf), for most people, the contracts are relatively standard and the ability to negotiate changes is sadly missing—although note that even with professional footballers, a contract is binding. Famously, Cristiano Ronaldo (paid over £100,000 a week at the time) claimed he was a 'slave' while being kept at Manchester United when he wanted a move to Real Madrid. We are all 'wage slaves' but some of us are better paid than others. It is also worth noting that some of the rights and responsibilities of a contract even extend beyond leaving formal employment, such as restrictive covenants, non-disclosure agreements, non-solicitation, and no poaching clauses. For example, sales people cannot take clients when they leave, and senior execs cannot work for competitors for a period of time.

Having a contract requires that it is operationalized. Contracts, even detailed ones, cannot envisage all potential circumstances and what every person is to do every minute for every day. This indeterminacy requires ongoing negotiation as managers seek to direct staff in their duties. This is because labour is embedded in people and is not a commodity, so any work done is volitional. This creates tensions and struggles over allocation of work, work pace, and issues of control more generally. A useful notion is that of the frontier of control, which is best thought of as a constantly renegotiated line. As things can move over time, the line changes through custom and practice, and becomes a new line. But equally, the line gets bent each day as part of this negotiation process.

The Covid-19 pandemic changed the norms concerning working at home and workers have in many cases been reluctant to return to the old normal with that rigidity and lack of flexibility. Some organizations are having to renegotiate a new normal.

This issue of indeterminacy is what has led to terms such as working without enthusiasm or work-to-rule being part of the language of the workplace—well before notions of engagement gathered currency in the workplace. Following orders can cause chaos too. In a famous novel by the Czech writer Jaroslav Hašek, *The Good Soldier Švejk*, the soldier—by doing exactly as he is told (taking orders literally)—causes mayhem in the Austrian army and exposes military stupidity (the ideas are similar to those espoused by Joseph Heller in *Catch 22*). While the satire was aimed at the army as a bureaucracy designed to organize people, the true/actual target is modern society; our elaborate structures and the people in power, who plan things without much awareness of how they will play out on the ground or how they affect ordinary people. Not surprisingly, *working without common sense* is also a term which is part of workplace language, reflecting exactly this point. Indeed a key issue with HRM is who implements it. While HRM may design policies (at the behest of senior managers), HRM is carried out by line managers, and the demands placed upon line managers in terms of adherence to rules may cause tension between them and the HR function.

Given the incompleteness of the employment contract, it is clear that all workers possess some 'tacit skills', that is, the knowledge and understanding workers accumulate throughout their lives, which is typically extremely difficult to write down into a contract or otherwise codify. Tacit skills can be seen in many areas of employment, such as in the ability to deal with people in various situations. While some skills can be copied by watching other people or reading handbooks, others must be 'learned' through practice or by doing similar jobs. The key thing, however, is that these skills and attributes are actually much more than 'simple common sense'.

A key point, as we will see later throughout the book, is that the employment relationship is a process of exchange, but that the exchange is political, within an unequal power relationship. This is often referred to as the asymmetry of power between capital and labour. In simple terms, ownership of production, an excess supply of job seekers, and the rights bestowed on managers through law, creates an uneven playing field. Some employees have more power than others (footballers more than architects, although a particular architect might have a high degree of bargaining power) and this may change over time. Employees can band together collectively through unions to bargain for better terms and conditions. Employers can move capital (factories etc.)

and set up somewhere else in a way which it is difficult for employees to do.

Much of my own work has drawn from an employment relations perspective where it is recognized that the relationship embodies both common and divergent interests. That is to say, both parties have interests in ensuring the organization performs well so that wages are paid and profit return to owners is satisfactory. However, there are also divergent interests. In simple terms, the employer is likely to wish to buy labour at the lowest possible price to maximize profits, whereas employees wish to sell their labour at the highest possible price. This produces a conflict of interest. Thus, it is best to understand that employment relations are dynamic. All this produces issues around what is termed the 'effort bargain'—what do I as the employee expend in terms of my effort in relation to the wage I get from my employer? Rationally, I could think of expending the minimum effort needed to keep my job. Why work harder? As Ronald Reagan said, 'hard work might not have killed anyone but why take the risk'. Actually, many people die of overwork, and the Japanese even have a word for it—'karoshi'. In fact, workers often collectively try to control how much work they all do to ensure there is no rate-busting individual working harder than their colleagues, which puts them all under pressure or threatens jobs. This is yet another illustration of conflicts of interest. In recent years, there has been talk of the need to find out how to get workers to expend discretionary effort—so rather than coerce them maybe find a way of eliciting their voluntary effort.

So HR can make work less dehumanizing (or more humanizing)—at least if done so more ethically or equitably by being pluralistic and inclusive. The Covid-19 pandemic raises issues such as what is the new workplace and how does HRM help make for better working lives?

Chapter 2
HRM: strategy and performance

Much of the interest in the contemporary HRM literature has been around its link with strategy. Premised on a larger organization and an actual HR department, the idea was that no longer was the HR unit to be in charge of office space, furniture, the first-aid kit, and the nuts and bolts of payroll, stationery, and finding new recruits but a newer, more important arena: developing and utilizing the potential of human resources in pursuit of the organization's strategic objectives.

This would entail a place on the management board and access at the highest level, rather than the HRM department being an organizational emergency service called in to clean up the fall-out of strategic decisions and ensuring that no one gets sued. Under old HRM thinking, the less anyone heard from the HRM department, the fewer problems there were. This reflected the preoccupation with labour as a problem and firefighting as the appropriate mode of action.

A famous quote is illuminating, noting a tendency in the past for the Human Resources department to be seen as a 'trash can' for all those tasks that do not fit anywhere else:

> Personnel administration … is largely a collection of incidental
> techniques without much internal cohesion. As personnel

administration conceives the job of managing worker and work, it is partly a file-clerk's job, partly a housekeeping job, partly a social worker's job and partly firefighting to head off union trouble or to settle it...the things the personnel administrator is typically responsible for...are necessary chores. I doubt though that they should be put together in one department for they are a hodgepodge...They are neither one function by kinship of skills required to carry out the activities, nor are they one function by being linked together in the work process, by forming a distinct stage in the work of the managers or in the process of the business.

From the 1980s onwards, the HRM literature and HRM departments talked of prioritizing strategy with HR people as business managers. In this scenario HRM departments and the people responsible for personnel management are at the centre of the action, helping the organization achieve its objectives, and are critical to the mission. Indeed, there is some evidence that senior management do think ahead systematically about managing people but also that this is fairly well downstream in organizational planning. Nevertheless, the importance of the management of people was to become much more central to management thinking about decisions which are related to creating and sustaining competitive advantage. And of course, in most organizations, strategies are shaped by forces beyond their immediate control (political, economic, social, and legal forces), which create the context for manoeuvre. Strategy can be seen as corporate strategy (the overall scope of the organization, its structures and financing, and the distribution of resources between its different constituent parts), competitive strategy (how the organization competes in a given market), and operational strategies (how the various sub-units such as marketing, finance, and including HRM contribute to the higher-level strategies).

The Anglo-American approach emphasizes shareholders as *the* key stakeholders and strategy is designed to primarily satisfy them, but other perspectives incorporate a much greater range of stakeholders that includes customers, local communities, the environment, workers, and societal expectations. HRM has to balance and indeed integrate the needs of employers, employees, and the wider society and should be guided by a moral and professional base. In short HRM requires social legitimacy for its work. Employers have a wider role in society, acting within legal norms, dealing with citizens and consumer groups, and, for example, they can contribute to the agenda of social inclusion and the health of the nation more generally. This wider perspective helps with the humanizing agenda.

Central to the modern HRM agenda was the importance of ensuring the commitment of employees across industry and a shift away from control. This fits with a movement towards the so-called 'soft aspects' of management style—shared values, staff, and skills. Commentators, including HRM advocates, argued that financial goals are not sufficient in themselves, but need to be underpinned by a broader set of societal values. In broad terms, the new HRM was seen as less bureaucratic, less concerned with administration, and more strategic, more integrated with business objectives, and substantially devolved to line managers, as part of an employee commitment perspective with the notion of employees as an asset, not a cost. Underlying this approach was the idea that HRM was not a series of individual policies, but an entire system that needed to be managed and fitted to overall organizational goals to achieve the desired outcomes.

As noted, one reason for the historical lack of emphasis on business strategy and HRM is that the HR function, or Personnel department, has traditionally never had a very prominent role in strategic development. Yet, however good the strategy, it needs to be successfully implemented and this depends on the effective management of human resources.

Just repeating the term 'strategy' and inserting it in every second sentence or at the top of every document does not make something strategic, and there is a danger of comparing an ideal type of HRM (strategic) with a descriptive view of personnel management (mundane). Despite some evidence of a greater emphasis on people management in corporate thinking and the growth in importance of the human resource management function, the function still has lower status and is accorded less significance than other functions (e.g. finance and marketing) and has tended to be ignored in business policy and strategic management texts.

A central problem for the HRM department is that they can occupy an ambiguous position within the organization, most commonly seen in their occupation of the middle ground between management and workers, but also because the employment relationship is contested. HRM is then a highly political activity and indeed often struggles to find a balance between commercial imperatives and employee well-being.

One way to get a handle on these issues is to think about hard or soft HRM. In simple terms, hard HRM is about 'fit', so HR is an asset like any other and a low-cost approach might mean HRM is about sweating the labour. In contrast, the 'soft' approach is based on the notion of 'resourceful humans' and people investment. This was nicely summed up by Harvard professor, Richard Walton, who refers to 'employees being given broader responsibilities, encouraged to contribute and helped to take satisfaction from work'.

But the management of human resources should be more than a mere consequence of strategy. Most business decisions will have some effects on the management of people, but such effects are not necessarily strategic decisions. Slashing the workforce in a kneejerk response to changes in profitability is simply a reactive decision, not a strategic one. We would expect to see very different strategies for the management of human resources from those organizations who see employees as a commodity, with the emphasis on cost control, while others may emphasize differentiation in terms of quality, with employees as a resource to be developed.

A more useful approach for us is to characterize strategic HRM as entailing strategic integration and a 'positive' approach to the management of employees with an emphasis on staff as a resource rather than a cost. Thus, strategic integration is a necessary but not sufficient component of strategic HRM. Equally, an emphasis on staff as a resource without strategic integration is not strategic HRM either. Developing staff in ways which are unrelated to the business strategy of the organization is not strategic HRM. In contrast, an 'accounting' view of labour management (that is, labour as a cost) may well be strategic in that it may be related to competitive advantage through cost leadership, and as such strategically integrated, but where human resources are simply sweated to create profit seems a far cry from bringing to life people as a key resource, which is what strategic HRM is supposed to be about. We suggest strategic HRM is about human resources actively contributing towards the organizational mission and not simply about not hindering existing business strategy. Of course, we may find that many organizations would fit neither category in that the management of staff may not be considered a strategic issue at all, nor be integrated into the strategic planning process, and staff may not be considered as a resource. In this sense, strategic HRM might apply to a minority of organizations while in others HRM might be more ad hoc, opportunistic, and reactive.

With this thinking organizations need to 'match' their human resource strategies to their business strategies, so that there is alignment. The configuration of practices that provides the tightest fit is then seen as being ideal for the particular strategy. This includes both horizontal fit between HR practices and vertical fit between HR practices and business strategy. Horizontal fit ensures the same messages are given out to staff as a result of HR practices being aligned. Thus, if long service is a key value, then this might override pay for performance. Or if the organization places high value on the voice and dignity of their workers, managers should not be rewarded for meeting performance targets, if they are achieved in a way that is inconsistent with these values. If the organization emphasizes innovation, HR practices should be supporting this with less of a compliance culture and even allowing for challenging voice and dissent. There are two major influential HR models: one being the Michigan model, which stresses a tight and calculative fit between business needs of the organization and management of people, and the other, the Harvard model (by Michael Beer and colleagues), which stresses the importance of multiple stakeholders and emphasizes people as a resource with well-being as an outcome as much as business performance. Here again we need to be reminded that an obsession with performance is problematic and that corporate metrics has a dehumanizing effect. Employee welfare is a vital role of HR, and getting too close to senior managers runs the risk of losing what is valuable about the HR function and its attention to other stakeholders.

Having said that, the extent to which human resource strategies can simply be 'matched' with the requirements of a changing business strategy, as if selecting a lounge suite, is open to question. The 'matching' literature has tended to assume that employee attitudes and behaviour can be moulded by management. Managers are the key designers and actors from this perspective. But human resource outcomes cannot be taken for granted. Indeed, the notion of best-fit is a rather static and perhaps an inappropriate metaphor in a rapidly changing world. Some strategy experts, drawing on behavioural science literature, argue that strategy in management suffers from 'chess syndrome', in that it is seen as a science of the intellect with analytical tools and strategic analysis at the forefront. But although, in chess, picking a move is intellectually complex, it is behaviourally trivial—once a move has been decided, making the move is simple and can happen instantly. However, execution or implementation in management is much trickier and is more expeditionary (like climbing Everest) than contemplative. Climbers of Everest have only two feasible moves to start, unlike chess in which there are 24 at the beginning and 10.9 million possible positions by move seven. Success in mountain climbing is not down to choosing which path to start with, but mastering the fundamentals, assembling and managing the right team of people, and anticipating and dealing with the conditions of the climb. This may well have value for the way we think about people in the organization, in that a motivated, engaged, and well-organized staff is likely to be of some importance regardless of the detail of strategy, which many employees, including managers, are unaware of. If this sounds exaggerated, an MIT study reported that less than one-third of executives and middle managers responsible for executing strategy could list three of their organization's strategic priorities.

Do we need to be concerned about strategy and HRM? One view is that since businesses exist to produce profit, not good HRM, and given that HRM practices are essentially facilitative and not stand-alone activities but must flow from corporate strategy, it is inevitable that they are not first order strategies. However, the danger here is to consider only first order strategies as really 'strategic', with other aspects dumped in the operational basket. This is misleading, as it assumes strategies are of one kind (assuming real strategy relates to product market issues) and other matters are either strategic or non-strategic, whereas we may be better thinking of *degrees* of strategy. Equally, a shareholder perspective places HR well downstream from the overall corporate mission, some might say drifting without the proverbial paddle, but even in the shareholder model (in which the business of business is business) there may be sense in thinking about how HR is not separate, but should be considered within the overall strategy. If you were setting up a new plant, as many Japanese firms did in the north-east of England in the 1980s, you would need to factor in (as they did) the skills the plant requires and the state of the labour market in that region before you started acquiring the land to build your factory.

Human resources need to be considered at two different levels. The first is at the level of implementation, where it is argued that much of the success of policy implementation depends on the effective management of human resources. The brilliant plan designed at the top is always going to be little more than a set of long documents outlining a future, which does not exist outside the boardroom, unless the work is translated or enacted on the ground. This requires line managers to take up the project, having both bought into the strategy and having the skills to carry it out. If we take a football analogy, not every team has the skills to play like today's Manchester City or the total football of the Dutch national team in the 1970s.

But there is also a case to be made that human resources need to be considered further up the planning process and to influence business strategy, so that rather than just flowing from the business strategy, they should be part of it. The human resource dimension may constrain the type of business strategy adopted or indeed provide opportunities. It is no good making a strategic business decision to relocate if the organization finds it cannot recruit a workforce, as noted above. Equally, the existing skills of the workforce may well constrain business growth.

In recent years, the HRM and strategy agenda has converged on a search for best practice. This is not new and can be traced back to Frederick Taylor and the scientific management era. HRM is not immune from a search for one best way either. In terms of the strategy we saw earlier, a best-fit approach is one where organizations, labour markets, technology, organization size and structure, national business and employment systems, product markets, and life cycle of the business are all potential influencing factors, and there is no single ideal set of practice to be employed in order to improve organizational performance. Others look at the nature of the strategy itself. Organizations operating at the top end of the market are likely to have different HR practices from those operating on a low-cost model, whether airlines (British Airways vs Ryanair) or restaurants (a luxury hotel such as The Ritz vs a fast food chain such as McDonald's), although even with the same market position there are different approaches, as we can see with the examples of Ryanair vs Southwest Airlines. There are also likely to be different HR issues that are important in different sectors—having a high staff turnover is more likely to be a problem for a firm of architects or management consultants than it is for a fast food chain.

In the 1990s, HR professionals finally appeared to have evidence that HR made a difference to organizational performance. Compelling evidence was accumulated to show a positive association between organizational performance and a bundle of complementary HRM practices, known collectively as high-performance work systems (HPWS). This bundle usually includes selective recruitment, extensive training, internal promotion, performance appraisals, work teams, and employee participation, among other practices. The positive association between HPWS and organizational performance holds in a wide range of studies conducted in many different countries. This universalistic 'best practice' evidence suggests that the HPWS bundle should be implemented widely. This recipe seems to apply across the board as good people management matters everywhere. The landmark 1996 study by the American HR scholar Mark Huselid on the Impact of Human Resource Management Practices on turnover and productivity showed that HPWS (he listed 13 practices) was significantly and positively related to lower staff turnover, higher profits, increased sales, and market value.

This new HRM paradigm fits with the notion that today, in modern organizations, the emphasis is on people not just working harder (sweating) but smarter, using their brains, knowledge, and skills rather than brawn and long hours to compete. Hence organizations should invest in people to deliver the best outcomes. As Western countries faced stiff competition from newly industrialized countries they had to move away from simple cost competition to competing on innovation and quality, which required HR investment. So these ideas married well with the demand for new ways of competing.

Much of the impetus for these ideas derives from the USA against the backdrop of a concern with the decline of US industry and how to turn around various sectors, especially manufacturing, with a high-skills model. But over time, the messages and the models spread into other sectors and then globally.

The core message was about bundles (simply, a collection of reinforcing HR practices) that facilitate worker participation and decentralize management, and that having a piecemeal take-up of HR practices means that organizations miss out on potential benefits. The task of the organization, and of HR managers in particular, is to identify an appropriate bundle for their organization and then implement such a high-performing work system.

However, this recommendation is rather easier to state than to follow. First, which HR practices should be included in these bundles? There is no definitive list, with some counting up to as many as 28. The original classic set is from Jeffrey Pfeffer, a Stanford Management Scholar. He lists seven 'universal' practices: employment security, selectivity in recruitment, high levels of contingent reward, self-managed teams, extensive training and development, information-sharing, and harmonization of status differentials. These are to be held together under an overarching philosophy with a long-term approach so that you have to invest to get the return.

This list needs to be adapted for the context of its application. Huselid's study included having an employee 'grievance' procedure as core best practice, for example, but in some countries this is simply the law, not evidence of best practice or leading-edge firms. Indeed, some of the fastest developing economies in the world have scant employment regulation and often rely on contracting workers from other countries, and rather than go through disciplinary processes might simply not renew the contract.

This is important given the US bent to the HRM literature, where there is little restriction on employment practices or the protection that one might find in the EU. But organizations are embedded in societies that influence them in a number of ways, including through the law/hard regulation, but also through their culture, codes of practice, and best practice. Organizations operate within national and institutional contexts and play within these national rules, which effectively provide a social licence to operate. So they do not have complete autonomy as they put together their HRM blueprint. Their strategic recipes are manufactured within this framework of hard and soft regulation.

While the research evidence on bundles reports positive associations, there are unresolved issues of causality. The major issue for these studies is that few use longitudinal data, so while there are numerous associations between HR practices and performance, we cannot be sure that these bundles lead to better performance because it is equally plausible that the organizations that perform better also have the resources to invest more in HR practice.

John Purcell, now Emeritus Professor at Bath University, issues a cautionary warning:

> The claim that the bundle of best practice HRM is universally applicable leads us into a utopian cul-de-sac and ignores the powerful and highly significant changes in work, employment and society visible inside organisations and in the wider community. The search for bundles of high commitment work practices is

important, but so too is the search for understanding of the circumstances of where and when it is applied, why some organisations do and others do not adopt HRM, and how some firms seem to have more appropriate HR systems for their current and future needs than others. It is only one of many ways in which employees are managed, all of which must come within the bounds of HRM.

In addition, and this is taken up in the next chapter, practices as preached are not the same as those implemented, let alone those experienced. The wonderful progressive set of practices listed in the HR strategy document may in fact be experienced rather differently by employees. What can be seen by those at the top of the organization as developmental performance management systems can be regarded by those further down as punitive. What HR might consider to be a clear articulation of culture and values can be seen by others as brainwashing. So, are we measuring the existence of the practice or the experience of it? Furthermore, to the extent that the data shows a link, we lack information on the processes involved. Scholars use the term 'opening up the black box' to indicate the need for detailed understanding of how practices might affect outcomes. In short, we have inputs and outputs, but what is the internal working? Why is there a relationship? What is it about having these specific sets of HR practices that delivers performance? What is the process by which these outcomes have occurred? One could copy a successful organization that has performance management with the same practice, but it is unlikely that simply implementing the same scheme will deliver benefits. Much will depend on the context of its introduction, the way it is implemented, the skills of the managers, the support provided by HR, and how it is perceived by employees.

An underlying basis for many of these ideas is the resource-based theory of the firm applied to management by Jay Barney, a US scholar. This suggests that competitive advantage depends on the organization having superior, valuable, rare, non-substitutable resources available and that these resources are not easily imitable. The latter is important as otherwise these resources could simply be copied and the advantage would be reduced or eliminated.

But the complexities and subtleties associated with organizational cultures and HRM practices cannot be simply transplanted by competitors. There is a complex interaction of HRM policies and an organization's 'social architecture', meaning skill-formation activities, cooperative behaviour, and the tacit knowledge an organization possesses. Looking at things from this perspective helps us understand why more organizations do not adopt these practices, as well as suggesting how simply adopting the latest fashions can sometimes barely scratch the surface of organizations.

But in all this we need to focus on the big picture. As Peter Boxall, Professor at the University of Auckland and one of the leading thinkers in HRM, observes, all organizations need some mix of HR practices to be able to do business; they need to recruit, train, and reward staff. In addition, the sort of practices will vary according to context, sector, their competitive strategy, and so on. The search for bundles is better seen as how to identify the sort of practices and principles that best support their goals. It is not very surprising that a universal bundle that works for all organizations, everywhere, does not exist. So, if we (both researchers and practitioners) abandon the notion of a one-best-way, we might be better off, and then we can spend more time identifying what sets of practices (or bundles) might be appropriate for which organizations.

The advance of technologies has had a major and disruptive impact on HRM. There are many new sophisticated technologies and consulting firms who have pre-packaged HR systems, which can use elaborate online ratings to reduce the need for judgement or expertise and can then marginalize HR departments. On the other hand, this might allow HR departments to move away from transactional or compliance work to allow a greater focus on using data to quantify and manage people in relation to organizational outcomes. Thus technology now exists to continuously monitor employees and track their performance (such as employed by Amazon and Walmart). And this technology is not just about workers in a warehouse but also those out and about, for example delivery drivers being monitored in real time by GPS, or even homeworkers sitting at home on their PCs in real time. We are all increasingly monitored—professional and semi-skilled, working in a physical location or remotely, with or without our knowledge. So higher profit can be secured not by people working smarter, but by sweating labour and using precarious and insecure forms of employment.

In short, strategy does matter and the new HRM has put this at the heart of the project. Integration, fit, and the notion of matching dominate the discussion. But this is not simply a matter of internal company dynamics; organizations are embedded in society and all that this entails in terms of laws, regulation, culture, and expectations. These create the context in which organizations operate, although of course organizations do not just have to be rule-takers but can lobby and attempt to change the rules of the game. So HR must operate within limits and cannot simply read off answers as if it were a simple technical solution. Moreover, the question of who is to be served—shareholders or a wider constituency of stakeholders—very much affects what kind of HRM we see. In the search for strategy we must also be mindful of the responsibilities of employers to employees.

Chapter 3
Who does HRM and how?

The practice of HRM is not something that resides solely in the hands of those who design HRM policies, namely senior managers and HR staff/departments. Whatever policies are designed by those at the top, others further down the ranks must implement them, even where there is an HR department to provide support and advice. Furthermore, these line managers are also responsible for many other operational matters and, in their list of priorities, HR is not always at the top. This is a perennial problem for line managers: the need to balance conflicting priorities within limited time constraints.

There is a large body of research that examines and explores the roles of different types of managers with distinctions made between middle managers, front-line managers, and supervisors, but here 'line manager' is used as a generic term, separating them out from senior management. Line managers *implement* HRM and the lived experience of HRM for most staff is provided by their line managers, hence the common saying that people join organizations but leave their bosses. It is also important to consider the gap between intended, actual, and perceived HR practices and not simply assume they are the same.

It is not then surprising that deviations (whether deliberate or planned) occur and inconsistencies appear in the treatment of staff within a single organization. With a greater awareness of line-manager roles, there is a new emphasis in the field of management in both the literature and the world of practice on these staff and the roles they play. Line managers are not simply carrying out orders—but bringing HR to life and exercising leadership in HR matters; not just using the skills that got them appointed to the role, which might not include how to manage staff effectively. There is growing evidence that people skills are becoming increasingly important. For example in the training of medical doctors technical ability is clearly important but medical treatment requires not just interaction between doctor and patient but the management of a team to ensure the best diagnosis and treatment. So, both technical and people management skills need to be built into training.

Before talking about strategy in practice we should note that the idea of a unified management strategy, designed by the chief executive and simply passed down the organization, is more than questionable. The development of strategy is more of an ongoing dialogue between different stakeholders and management functions. It is also sensible to see organizations as inherently pluralistic, which itself implies potential resistance (and renegotiation) of new human resource strategies from groups of employees and sections of management.

There is a danger that when HRM policy decisions are made, implementation is regarded as a simple operational matter to be left to the HR department. This is a mistake as line managers need to understand their critical role as the link between the strategic direction of the organization and the management of front-line staff members.

In one organization where I conducted research, there was a realization that there was little point in producing corporate plans that envisaged major strategic changes unless staff were committed to implementing them. As one senior manager put it:

'It was beginning to register amongst management that unless the staff were up to scratch and on-board with change, the bank was not going to get there.'

In assessing HR practice, we need to look particularly at the relationship between HR and the line manager. This is tricky as HR is criticized both for being too interventionist and rule bound but also too remote and out of touch with the realities and dynamics of the workplace. For example, a line manager might want hard non-negotiable rules at times and at other times flexibility and will rail against HR for not giving them what they want in both cases. This is not a case of fickle line managers but a pragmatic response to their specific but varied circumstances. For example, when struggling with a difficult employee who takes up a lot of their time a manager might seek a hard and fast rule to remove their own discretion so as to limit the conversation. Far better (from a relationship and stress viewpoint) to be sadly and apologetically applying some non-negotiable HR rule than to have a lengthy and what they might see as difficult conversation in which the manager acknowledges that they have the responsibility and discretion, but are choosing not to exercise it. On the other hand, on other occasions the manager might want to exercise their own discretion in cases where there is a hard and fast rule.

A good example of this can be seen in a study of performance management (PM) in the civil service in which the front-line managers focused on completing what they saw as the *compulsory* components of the formal PM system (filling in the forms) as a signal that they were conforming to the system, but then preferred to write up positive reports of staff whose work needed improvement, while confining their actual views to informal conversations with the staff member: 'I will tell them personally...Of course, I cannot say something bad about my subordinates, as it reflects on the whole team and our work. So, normally I won't say anything bad about them during the appraisal.'

By appearing to comply with the intended system, these managers try to keep control of their work units and manage the expectations of their employees without interference by the HR department or senior managers. The actions are not ad hoc but are to ensure they maintain flexibility managing their work group and keeping other organizational actors happy within the system. Thus front-line managers need to balance the different demands and expectations of other organizational actors. For HR in this instance, a set of completed forms counts as the performance outcome, and the line managers duly delivered this.

In recent years, line managers have taken on greater responsibility for HR activities, although usually working together with HR or senior managers. In some areas, legal issues such as those around recruitment, selection, and discipline constrain how much can be devolved to them. There are several issues that affect the way line managers cope with HR responsibilities, influencing what they do, and if they are to function effectively these issues need to be understood and addressed by senior managers in the organization.

The first issue is that line managers or supervisors do not always identify very much with organizational goals as handed down by senior managers. They often see themselves as stuck in the middle and, of course, they actually spend more time with co-workers than with senior managers. So 'them and us' can be employees and middle managers against senior managers rather than managers together against employees. Physical distance also creates a 'them and us' culture, where senior managers are divorced from the shop floor (ordering troops from far away from the danger) and unaware of the day-to-day workload, which may not bear much resemblance to the mental model senior managers have of what is or should be happening.

There are also other issues related to differing perspectives in relation to how management should be carried out. Line managers coming up through the ranks can have a hard-nosed view of staff they manage and a sceptical view of managers out of university who may not have spent time on the shop floor. In a project some years ago, a supervisor complained of idealistic views of workers held by these new innocent and 'unblooded' managers and suggested that rather than dabbling with concepts about involving staff in decision-making, providing for voice opportunities, and other progressive ideas, a branding iron was a much more useful tool to be used in the workplace.

Line managers can feel not just stuck between conflicting demands and stakeholders but squeezed and rather more victims than agents of change. Indeed, with new performance management techniques managers are under greater pressure to perform and discretion has declined as the work performance is now much more visible to their superiors. Quarterly reports are replaced by daily, if not hourly, updates and managers can feel much more scrutinized. One can see how middle managers can feel pressured from above and below, given employees can now be more questioning of middle managers' decisions. Some have argued that the loyal 'organization man' of the type described by William Whyte in his book of the same name (1956) has been replaced by managers who are more measured in their commitments and with more awareness of their disposability. Others have argued that the middle management role is being transformed rather than replaced, with more demanding work but also greater personal autonomy, and increased skill levels.

In one study branch managers in a bank complained that they have accountability but not authority:

> 'So, the problem is we are faced with enquiries at the counter, which cannot be resolved at the counter. They must be resolved through phone calls and memos. That causes frustration with me; it causes frustration with our cashiers. We are losing a little bit of the autonomy we used to have, but we are actually gaining the responsibility. We carry the can for it without being able to do anything about it.'

They were also frustrated by the bureaucratic rules governing their decision-making:

> 'One of the biggest problems in branches is that people decide things at head office and you think, "they have never been in a branch". It's a totally different working atmosphere. To put things into practice at branch level that are thought up at head office is often a frustrating process. It's bloody irritating to think that the people who thought this one up have never been facing a customer and solving their problems.'

Other managers referred to the feeling of standing between senior management and staff:

> 'I find it difficult in some ways because I've seen the management side of things and I've seen the workers' side of things, and what I've got to do as a manager is to keep staff happy, when perhaps I'm not all that happy myself…'

The clear gap between senior managers' vision of the future and the attitudes of middle management reflects fundamentally conflicting views as to the appropriateness of the policy. So middle management are sometimes implementing, but not always in a committed fashion, policies which they regard as neither desirable nor practical.

Competing priorities and work overload are other problems to be faced. Central to understanding how policies are implemented is that one must distinguish between formal and operational policy. Formal policy relates to the official statements (verbal or written) of top-level management. In contrast, operational policy relates to how senior management order policy priorities. So, simply put, where do we want staff to spend their time? More of one thing usually means less of something else. If senior managers fail to make the choice, line managers have to work out what the actual rather than the espoused priorities are.

According to the work of Edgar Schein on organizational culture and leadership, official policy and mission statements are much less important than the role-modelling of senior managers and how they reward and punish their employees through pay and promotion. If managers get rewarded for meeting targets, even if they are achieved by bullying their staff, although the official values promote well-being and respect, then these official statements are perhaps more useful being recycled as wrapping paper for fish and chips than being plastered to the walls of HQ. Managers (and employees) pick up these signals as to which are the *real* values and what is lip service, and there are many studies showing that production goals and sales targets are the trump cards. For example, despite pressures and changing public and company discourses over work–life balance, productivity and performance are still considered to be the leading priorities.

Given this, HR work can be regarded as extra work that is a nuisance, to be ticked off as hurriedly as possible, or even ignored, if line managers do not feel they are being monitored. If there is enhanced scrutiny then cynical managers can quickly resurrect some old apparatus to show they have been doing what senior managers want or expect; the quickly convened away-day that ticks many boxes vis-à-vis strategy (we talked about stuff), team-building (group hugs), and engagement (they all turned up), even if not much happens as a result and the potential benefits are often weakened from the outset by instructions to only speak positively (moving forward) and not to marinate over past failings/ problems. Senior staff who are responsible for one aspect of work assume their priorities are the same as those of the line manager. They assume line managers have one list and their task is at the top. One line manager neatly responded to an urgent request with: 'it's at the top of one of my lists', as a response to the need to balance conflicting priorities within limited time constraints.

In other research conducted in hospitals, where managers have a wide range of responsibilities, they can feel overwhelmed by their normal work so try to cut back on HR tasks, which are seen as a lower priority than tasks to do with patient care, and are left until there is more time—and there is always more urgent work to attend to—until they get a hard prompt.

Another major issue is that line managers often do not possess the skills and competencies that are needed to carry out the HR dimensions of their jobs as intended by senior managers. Few managers have undertaken any formal training in HRM before they become managers and they are often promoted on the basis of their good work in a lower-level role which may not have involved HR duties. Furthermore, the constant work pressure limits the training they are given.

'I got here accidentally [laughter]. I have no idea (how I became Ward Manager). I transferred from a surgical ward to this department at the request of my DoN (Director of Nursing), and I transferred as a level two nurse, and the next day, I was to assume a 2IC [second-in-command] type role…The next day the nurse manager, well his wife, had a baby and he went on paternity leave and basically never came back, so I got stuck here' (Ward Manager).

'I basically worked on the wards for a couple of years, then became a clinical nurse, so was in charge of shifts and whatever, at the time the manager that walked on the ward went into the back and there was no one else to step up so I went from being a clinical person to suddenly managing a ward, and unfortunately in nursing school they don't teach you how to do that, they teach you how to be a nurse, but they don't teach you about budgets, about people management, about anything, so that's been a real deficit…I think I was probably lucky because I had a good mentor, that helped me identify what I needed to work on and without that mentor I wouldn't have gotten to where I am' (Director of Nursing).

Despite their lack of experience and training, line managers are not always keen to sign up to do training. There are several reasons for this. One is they are often too busy to take part in courses; the second is they regard HR as common sense; and the third is a rather negative view of HR work. A negative view of HRM work was apparent in one chemical company where we were told that the well-established view was that 'bosses are bosses and kick ass'. This was a view strongly held by supervisors in the factory, who referred to the 'hairy arsed culture', and there were anecdotes of workers urinating in each other's tea mugs. Supervisors saw themselves as 'muscular types'—not necessarily with 'fine feelings'. Running a tight ship was not seen as being aided in any way by devoting time pandering to a 'long haired idealistic view of workers' from university graduates. Given their perception that workers only wanted to 'take, take, take', their apprehension was that what managers saw as progressive management was simply 'soft'. Thus 'we're going softly, softly, but we need the big sticks to come out as well'.

This view of HRM as common sense is not simply line management myopia; often senior managers share a similar willingness to ignore expertise, confident of spotting talent and keen to override recruitment and selection processes as they feel they know better.

The flow diagram (Figure 2) presents a clear pictorial representation of the steps in the HRM process and illustrates the several points in between the intended HRM policies and behavioural or performance outcomes.

In following this flowchart, we can see that intended policies are not the same as the ones implemented. Indeed, there is often a large gap between policy and practice in HRM. For example, in a study of a hospital it was noted that although the HR policy on bullying reflected best practice, its implementation was uneven as

| Intended HRM policies |
| These are designed by senior management as part of HR strategy, and may be publicised through mission statements |

| Implemented HR practices |
| This indicates the extent to which intended policies are actually put into effect by line managers, reflecting the reality of HRM at workplace level |

| Perceived HR practices |
| This is the way in which HRM is viewed and experienced by those in non-managerial roles or lower down the hierarchy |

| Worker attitudes |
| This reflects the attitudes workers hold towards work and their jobs, such as job satisfaction, organisational commitment, trust and loyalty |

| Behavioural outcomes |
| This reflects the behaviours that flow from these attitudes, reflected in factors such as absenteeism, labour turnover, sabotage or participation in industrial action |

| Performance outcomes |
| Outcomes such as product quality and customer service, which can apply both at an individual or team level, or those at a more distal level such as profits and productivity |

2. A graphical representation of the HRM–performance link.

line managers chose to give priority to other aspects of their work and put bullying into the 'too hard' basket. This resulted in persistent high levels of bullying, which affected staff well-being and performance. Research suggests, therefore, that it is misleading to look at HR practices alone, as even the 'best HR practices' are unsuccessful unless implemented effectively.

As noted earlier, managers prefer flexibility on when to apply rules. While HR can see the value of consistency in terms of values and policies (and compliance with employment legislation) managers value the ability to make informal deals to manage their world. Hard rules, which they cannot nuance, reduce their ability to negotiate with staff or even reward those they cannot pay more, or of whom they have asked an extra favour (e.g. taking on a tricky job at short notice, covering for an absent employee, etc.), such as giving them time off, or allowing them to take an afternoon off to take their child to football.

Here, policies that have been designed by HR to ensure uniformity and consistency can be seen from the line manager's perspective rather differently, as a silly bureaucratic rule to keep HR in work, bossing everyone else while not adding value to the business. So HR cannot merely produce policy but must open dialogue with line managers so that there is some understanding of how custom and practice can set like concrete and create problems. Concomitantly line managers need to acknowledge the costs of getting HR decisions wrong in terms of legal costs and negative publicity and value the protective role of HR.

If these new HR policies are implemented, how might they be perceived by employees? If line managers can be sceptics, then so can employees. Thus, grand plans designed from the top can often wash through the shop floor without leaving much of a trace, with line managers and other staff both sharing some scepticism of the higher management vision. The nature of the hype changes regularly and long-serving employees have seen it all before with new managers launching grand new initiatives as the great leap forward while conveniently erasing previous experiences from discussion. Early work within the field of HRM neglected non-managerial employees, focusing primarily on value to the organization, but there has been something of a corrective recently, with a growing interest in understanding the effects such systems have on employee outcomes, particularly outcomes related to employee well-being. Clearly, we need to focus more on the way HR practices are perceived and experienced by employees in order to better understand the effect of HRM on individual and organizational outcomes.

Whatever the grand vision and rolling prose with catchy phrases and jargon, employees are not dupes. Their approach to work may reflect ambition or pride in their work as much as (or instead of) a belief in the organization itself. Workforces will interpret, evaluate, and make their own independent audit of management. They may not be resistant to change but resistant to change which they see as having negative consequences for them, such as intensification. Thus, although not being able to challenge the 'logic' of management action in principle, they still have abilities to respond in other ways. Employees do not simply lap up corporate speak, nor do they follow orders like military personnel. Cooperation may be only temporary or conditional. One senior manager in an organization we visited referred to the 'monster' effect, in that employees' compliance related to their being fearful for their jobs. Sometimes there are deeply held views of work relationships. At this same organization, we were told there was a fundamental distrust based on 'people being divided into bears (workers) and gaffers (management), and the bears don't trust the gaffers'. So while there was considerable management communication this was not well received but was seen as propaganda. Messages received by employees may not be the ones management think they are sending out.

Worker attitudes are important. Sometimes effective, self-motivated workers are best left alone. A fascinating study of slaughtermen showed that these workers were self-motivated and indeed governed themselves, admittedly at times in rather unpleasant ways (spraying blood over each other), but they worked best with management not overlooking them. Sometimes less management is more, or at least better for productivity.

For employees coping with management ideas they find facile, there are many possible behavioural responses. Ben Hamper's account of his time at General Motors (GM) in the Flint, Michigan factory (the subject of the Michael Moore movie *Roger and Me*), showed a factory under pressure to raise quality standards to compete with Japanese companies. GM had a cat mascot to promote quality, 'howie makem', who patrolled the factory, exhorting workers to produce higher quality. Employees responded by having a 'quantity cat' (another mascot) which they thought more accurately represented GM values and the quantity cat duly chased 'howie makem' away.

More damaging examples of employees getting back at management can be seen in a British Airways (BA) dispute in the 1990s in relation to cost cuts affecting cabin crew. In a bitter dispute, cabin crew staff were warned not to strike, and BA managers told staff that those taking industrial action would be sacked and then sued for damages. Those who simply stayed away would face disciplinary action, be denied promotion, and lose both pension rights and staff discounts on flights for three years. BA were also reported to be filming picket lines. The subsequent strike ballot saw 73 per cent of employees voting in favour of strike action and a series of 72-hour strikes. BA had temporary staff and 'volunteer managers' to carry out ground handling staff duties and prior to the first day of action these managers rang cabin crew at home telling them 'they had a duty to cooperate with their employer'. On the first scheduled day of action only 300 workers declared themselves officially on strike but more than 2,000 called in sick. (This is similar to what is known in the USA as blue flu when police officers simultaneously take sick leave as an alternative to strike action.) Collective industrial action was expressed as collective illness. The strike was costly and bitter. An undercover employee publication gave clues on how to delay aircraft such as throwing duvet feathers into the engine, supergluing down the toilet seat, and poisoning the pilot:

'a particularly obnoxious captain can be made to suffer all the symptoms of violent food poisoning by emptying eye drops from the aircraft medical kit into his salad or drink'.

A more recent example comes from the experience of supermarket workers in the USA during the coronavirus crisis, studied by Alex Wood. Despite the vital role of such workers, respect seemed to be in short supply and workers faced 'workplace despotism' with threats of dismissal. His informants explained that managers could do 'whatever they want to do to whoever' especially in relation to altering work hours, which was used as a form of 'flexible discipline'. The power of scheduling required workers to curry favour with managers in order to receive 'schedule gifts', that is more or better hours. As one worker noted:

> 'You are just wondering like, "Oh my God, are they going to change my hours, are they going to cut my hours next week, am I going to have enough money for my rent next week?"'

However, workers found ways to get back at management. For example, one worker secretly rotated all the store's milk supplies so those going off first were at the back of the refrigerator, causing the loss of over £500-worth of milk and the sanctioning of the manager by his superiors.

These cases might be more extreme and colourful, but they are useful correctives to the idea that everyone shares the same perspectives on the state of HRM in their organizations. In a recent comparative study of the USA and Australia managers reported a more positive outlook than their employees, with the largest gap, in both countries, being in the assessment of collaborative/commitment management style. Perhaps this is not a major surprise as a manager's idea of collaboration might be rather different from that of an employee, and it is also probably not a surprise to find that on nearly all measures, senior managers (employers) gave higher scores on aspects of HRM than employees. It is true that managers tend to believe they are good leaders and communicate well (illusory superiority principle), however, the rating is not just about themselves, but about relations with employees where one might expect to see a less rosy picture. One perspective might put greater trust in managerial views given their broader perspective, but another might say that HRM is only part of their overall set of responsibilities, and a second order one at that, whereas employees' lived experience provides more accurate ratings.

In the final section of the flowchart model there are performance outcomes such as quality or customer service. Often it is best to look at these at unit or work group level as this is a more meaningful measure of how workers might be able to contribute to improved performance. So we might look at the links between levels of employee satisfaction and customer satisfaction, for example, rather than a more distal measure such as profitability, over which most workers may have very little influence.

In looking at line managers' implementation of HRM, it is evident that the process of human resource management is complicated and problematic and is best looked at through the prism of pluralism: this means being sensitive and unsurprised by the differing perspectives between the various levels and functions of management, as well as between the top management 'mission' and the aspirations of ordinary employees. Strategy emerges through the interplay between various management and employee stakeholders, and it is modified as a result of this process.

Chapter 4
Managing performance and rewards

The subject of reward management and performance is usually seen as being concerned with the matter of pay, and indeed this is a key component of HRM. How many of us are going to continue to remain in our jobs without the promise of a pay packet? A traditional view would be to see pay as simply the expected arrangement in compensating employees for turning up to work, so an employer would do little more than pay the 'going rate' as part of the simple exchange of money for labour. However, increasingly pay and reward are now seen as key levers to elicit effort and performance, and it is not simply the amount of money but how that money is paid that is important. This perspective, the so-called 'new pay' approach—a term coined by the American management theorist Ed Lawler—regards pay as part of a strategic choice employers make rather than simply a reflection of laws or environmental or market pressures. If one takes a long-term perspective on the reward literature, what is striking is the growing emphasis on reward as a strategic tool to influence corporate values and beliefs and effect organizational performance. The concept of 'New Pay' uses reward to link business strategy and the behaviours required to achieve it. The reward strategy is to be designed to reflect the organization's goals, values, and culture, and New Pay is about identifying pay practices that enhance the organization's strategic effectiveness.

However, it is worth noting that although many organizations claim to have a compensation or reward policy, rather fewer have this written down and fewer still have enacted it. Although this is frequently discussed (as a 'strategic compensation' or 'strategic rewards'), the extent to which rewards are actually used as a strategic tool in practice is rather more open to question.

In the New Pay model, the reward system signals to employees the importance their employer places on various activities or behaviours. For example, reward systems that provide benefits to long-serving staff are likely to shape the existing culture into one in which loyalty is seen as central to the corporate values. In contrast, at the now notorious Enron, an ex-trader said: 'if I am on the way to my boss's office talking about compensation, and if I can stomp on someone's throat on the way and that doubles it, well then I'll stomp on the guy's throat'. As Steven Kerr, an American scholar, noted many years ago in a famous article titled 'On the folly of rewarding A, while hoping for B', whether dealing with monkeys, rats, or human beings, 'it is hardly controversial to state that most organisms seek information concerning what activities are rewarded, and then seek to do (or at least pretend to do) those things, often to the virtual exclusion of activities not rewarded'.

It is nevertheless sensible to examine what management understands or assumes motivates people as they design their systems on that basis. Equally, employees need to think through what expectations they have of work, including reward. Ultimately, incentives have to be based on what employees value, as was noted by economists: it is the fish who decide what is the bait, and sometimes you need to ask the fish what they prefer to nibble on. Of course, these days we might be more sophisticated: it is not what the fish say (they may simply provide the answers they believe are expected of them) but it is their *behaviour* that tells you what they want.

Do we work to live or live to work? In one recent study, work was regarded as one of the worst activities for people's momentary happiness—just above being sick in bed (see Table 1 in Chapter 1). In other words, work can drain our happiness. Indeed, the term used in the USA for reward is often 'compensation', which evokes an underlying philosophy that pay is compensation for something that has caused harm—an accident, death, or disaster. So, work can be regarded as a similarly traumatic event requiring compensation for the daily indignity inflicted upon us when we give up time to be at the disposal of someone else as a result of the need to earn a crust, which is the fate of most of us who have not won the lottery or become independently wealthy.

A lot of research on reward begins with trying to understand human motivation. Classically, there are content and process theories, with the former based on the idea of fundamental human needs such as shelter or food, whereas the latter is based on the psychological processes involved. The legacy of these ideas remains strong: the father of scientific management, F. W. Taylor, saw workers as rational economic beings, but lazy and needing to be motivated; hence the importance of designing payment-by-results schemes to align management and worker interests. However, such an approach can become self-fulfilling. As William Whyte pointed out, managers assume workers and machines are passive agents who must be stimulated by management to get anything out of them. He noted that with machines they turn on the electricity whereas with workers they use money. The assumption underlying much of this thinking is that without incentives, financial or otherwise, workers are prone to swing the lead (a nautical expression from when sailors dropped lead lines to check water depth but on occasion would simply swing the line over the water and call out a fictitious depth). Workers are active agents in the process and respond to action or inaction, as in the saying that managers pretended to pay us and we pretended to work...

Taylor's ideas were not uncontested and the Human Relations School developed the notion of 'social man' to contrast with Taylor's 'economic man'. The basis of their thinking was rooted in the famous experiments at the Hawthorne works of General Electric where 30,000 workers were employed on assembly lines producing telephone equipment. These experiments were set up to examine the productivity associated with better lighting. The early findings were hopeful in that as lighting improved so did productivity but, disappointing senior managers who were desirous of the message that more lighting is better, productivity also improved in the other teams where lighting stayed the same or, indeed, was dimmed to the point that it was too dark to see what they were doing. Although GE general managers thought this was of little value to them, those involved in the project decided to extend the experiment to study work behaviour in relation to rest breaks, hours of work, pay schemes, and other conditions such as room temperature and humidity.

The original findings were interpreted as the result of bringing workers together and allowing them more input into work, as well as the effect of being observed, which became known as the Hawthorne effect (the very act of being watched changes the behaviour you wish to observe). But the Human Relations School also noted that workers did not always respond to incentive schemes in the way that managers had expected, often having their own goals (as a group) that acted against management. This notion that workers have other objectives is often forgotten. In 1952 Donald Roy conducted a famous participant observation study that demonstrated that workers who soldiered (restricted output) did so not because they lacked understanding of the 'economic logics of management'; they were well aware of their own economic interests, but they saw them as being different from those of managers. The workers' group decided that, if they overworked and received excess earnings, management would re-time the work and cut the piece-rate. They used social norms to keep people from busting the rate.

3. Maslow's hierarchy of needs.

Other models have been fashionable over time and have some narrative appeal, even if the empirical evidence for their value is rather shaky, as in the case of Maslow's 'hierarchy of needs' (Figure 3) with the notion that people satisfy one particular need (physiological needs, safety needs, belonging and love, social needs, esteem needs, and then self-actualization) before moving on to try to satisfy the next in the ordered hierarchy. The evidence supporting the notion of a universal hierarchy of needs is thin as is the notion that we work steadily up the hierarchy. For example employees may demand not only more money but also more satisfying work at the same time. As Edgar Schein commented, we have to deal with complex man rather than economic or social man (*sic*) and complex man has many motives that are arranged in some sort of hierarchy of importance but this is subject to change from time to time and situation to situation. Equally, Herzberg's influential two-factor theory of motivation posits that satisfaction and dissatisfaction are not necessarily related, with the insight that just because a person did not feel satisfied about a particular aspect of their work did not mean they were necessarily dissatisfied. Equally, if workers were not dissatisfied that did not imply automatic satisfaction. The motivators associated with good feeling included the work itself, achievement, responsibility,

50

recognition, and advancement, whereas 'hygiene' factors associated with bad feeling included pay, working conditions, and supervision. Unless hygiene factors are satisfied, motivation is of little use. As Herzberg saw it, managers do not need to motivate employees by giving them higher wages, more benefits, or newer status symbols. Rather employees are motivated by their own inherent need to succeed at a challenging task. The manager's job then is not to motivate people to get them to achieve; instead, the manager should provide opportunities for people to achieve so they will become motivated.

Many years later, Alfie Kohn in his book *Punished by Rewards* (1993) argued that studies show that intrinsic interest in a task (the sense that something is worth doing for its own sake) tends to decline when the individual concerned is given an external reason for doing it. Extrinsic motivations are not only less effective than intrinsic motivations, they can also corrode or crowd out intrinsic motivation. People who work in order to get a reward tend to be less interested in the task than those who are not expecting to be rewarded. According to Kohn, when we do something in order to get a prize, we feel that the goal of the prize controls our behaviour, and this deprivation of self-determination makes tasks seem less enjoyable. Moreover, the offer of an inducement sends a message that the task cannot be very interesting; otherwise it would not be necessary to bribe us to do it. Kohn pointed out that much of the work on motivation drew from captive audiences, such as children at school or prison inmates who had limited room for manoeuvre and could be easily manipulated. Even here, the idea of motivation through incentives proved problematic, with schoolchildren being given rewards on reading (measured by the number of books they borrowed from the library) eliciting a subversive response: checking out books without reading them. When this led to teachers testing them on what they had read, they borrowed shorter books or those with more pictures. This might cause us to think that if small children can subvert measurement systems, then perhaps motivated adults might have the wit to game the system too. The intrinsic/extrinsic motivation debate was revived with the bestselling book *Drive* by Daniel Pink, which stresses the importance of mastery, meaningfulness, and autonomy in creating motivation.

Equally, it is hard to dispute that money matters, but is it simply the total amount of money or is it money relative to what others earn? We tend to be more exercised by our close colleague being paid more than ourselves than we do by people up the road doing the same job. How about if work is more enjoyable—would we trade off money for enjoyment? How about those who earn more than they can spend: is this about recognition of worth? And how about activity, variety, status, and social contacts? These are all issues in the reward domain. Reward clearly does have an emotional component.

During Covid-19, as farmers were concerned that labour shortages (caused by lack of migrant labour) meant crops might be lost and with locals reluctant to move the long distances involved because of concerns with low pay and working conditions, the Deputy Prime Minister of Australia, Michael McCormack, tried to counterbalance these negative perceptions by appealing to young Australians to move to the country to pick fruit because it is a 'great Instagram moment'.

In the last 30 years we have seen a mantra, or loaded narrative, around 'pay for performance', and it might seem self-evident that the deserving, hard-working employees (ourselves) should be paid more than undeserving slackers or those who put more time into impressing management and grandstanding than actually doing the work (others). However, there is nothing new in the concept of paying for performance. Payment by results aims to establish a direct link between reward and effort. Such schemes reflect the ideas of F. W. Taylor, who, by standardizing work processes through time and motion studies, laid the groundwork for such schemes to operate and saw piecework as a way by which workers could see a clear link between their individual effort and earnings. While popular in textiles, this type of pay has declined in recent years although commission payments to sales staff continue this tradition. Plays such as *Death of a Salesman* and *Glengarry Glen Ross* showed something of the dynamics of these high-pressure sales environments on the stage and in films. We saw how this worked on a personal level when we tried to get quotes on double glazing. My parents decided it made sense to get the sales people from three different companies to come the same afternoon, not realizing that they were hard to budge, and by 6 p.m. three sales people all with special offers only for today and all with their wives' birthday had to be manoeuvred out of the house by my more assertive brother, who had to drive over to do the eviction.

Still, the popularity of such incentive structures was badly dented by scandals over the mis-selling of pensions in the 1990s in the UK, with payment by commission considered to be a major contributor to problems with customers encouraged to buy products not in their interest so that staff got their commission payments. In response to the backlash, some companies pulled their staff off the road and re-examined their sales incentives. More recently the PPI (payment protection insurance) scandal in the UK emerged with up to 3 million people having been sold ineffective schemes by sales people chasing commissions and producing high profits for the banks. In Australia, the Banking Royal Commission in 2019 unearthed the 'Dollarmites Scandal', where staff created accounts, either using their own money or that of the bank, to meet their targets for opening accounts for children.

Some argue that incentive payments (or commission) are more suitable for routine tasks such as installing windshields: the subject of a famous study by Ed Lazear, in which piece-rates replaced hourly wages and led to productivity increases of 40 per cent. But there are the dangers of unintended consequences: Domino's ended its guarantee of delivering pizza within 30 minutes after multi-million-dollar settlements arose from car accidents involving its delivery drivers. The official line was that this was not a result of drivers going too fast to meet the target, but the guarantee was dropped in an attempt to fight a 'public perception of reckless driving and irresponsibility'. The more recent manifestation of these pressures can be seen in the stories of delivery drivers for Amazon, Hermes, and the like who as self-employed drivers (independent contractors) are unpaid for non-deliveries and resort to creative methods such as leaving the parcel with a dog or putting parcels through toilet windows.

There is also an example concerning an HR officer who was told to reduce turnover in his department. To achieve the bonus, he changed the hiring criteria to simply find candidates who were the least likely to leave. Rather than focus on their suitability for the role, he transferred problem employees to other departments, gave unsuitable employees five chances, and altered the method of calculating the turnover ratio.

Even in the context of the police service, targets passed down the chain of command from the commissioner to constables (with promotion linked to meeting such targets) saw officers recording fewer crimes by recording thefts as 'lost property', burglaries as 'theft from property', and attempted burglaries as 'criminal damage' to enable targets to be met.

Incentives are very much hard-wired into modern management thinking, reflecting Adam Smith's famous words that:

> It is not from the benevolence of the butcher, the brewer, or the baker, that we expect our dinner, but from their regard to their own self-interest.

Ironically, most people do not think they will respond to the same incentives that they expect others to respond to: I am only interested in doing worthwhile work whereas everyone else is

John Crace on selling and reselling

Back in the early 1990s, when I reached my mid-30s, I finally got around to taking out a personal pension. With my customary inattention to detail, I did next to no research on what the best pension might be and duly signed on the dotted line with the same financial adviser that my friend Alex had used. On a couple of occasions early on, as I earned a little more, I increased my monthly contributions but other than that I barely gave my pension a moment's thought. The most recent annual statement informed me that I could expect to retire with a pension of less than £5,000 per year. So I was amazed to get an email from the financial adviser who had sold me the pension, someone I had not spoken to for over 25 years, informing me that the pension he had sold me might not have been ideal and might technically be described as having been mis-sold. He was, however, no longer working for the company and had moved to a firm that specialized in getting compensation for people who had been mis-sold pensions. Would I like him to act on my behalf to recover the money from the pension, which he might have mis-sold?

motivated by chasing more money. In fact, research suggests that having people chase money gets them to be good at chasing money. Managers often immediately turn to incentives as a lever for change, even if previous experience is mixed; but changing dials from a distance is easier and less messy than managing face to face. Indeed, it is not uncommon that an organization wants to change their incentives because of dissatisfied staff, but if they were to dig deeper, the actual reason usually relates to poor management or issues to do with senior management themselves.

Jeffrey Pfeffer, the US management scholar, provides a valuable corrective to some of the common ideas about pay (see Table 2).

Table 2. Myths about reward

Myth	Reality
Labour rates and labour costs are the same thing.	They are not. Labour rates are wages divided by time. Labour costs are a calculation of how much a company pays its people and how much they produce. Thus, German factory workers may be paid at a rate of $30 an hour and Indonesians $3, but the workers' relative costs will reflect how many widgets are produced in the same period of time.
You can lower your labour costs by cutting labour rates.	Labour costs are a function of labour rates and productivity. To lower labour costs, you need to address both. Indeed, sometimes lowering labour rates increases labour costs.
Labour costs constitute a significant proportion of total costs.	Labour costs as a proportion of total costs vary widely by industry and company.
Low labour costs are a potent and sustainable competitive weapon.	It may be better to achieve competitive advantage through quality; through customer service; through product, process, or service innovation; or through technology leadership.
Individual incentive pay improves performance.	Individual incentive pay undermines performance—of both the individual and the organization. Many studies strongly suggest that this form of reward undermines teamwork, encourages a short-term focus, and leads people to believe that pay is not related to performance at all but to having the 'right' relationship and an ingratiating personality.
People work for money.	People do work for money, but they also work for meaning in their lives.

In recent years much of the discussion around reward has been to do with performance-related pay, and is more about white-collar managerial and professional staff. Rather than pay for service or loyalty (as with teachers or civil servants), the aim was to introduce more commercialism with a narrative around 'paying for performance'. With these schemes, pay is linked to performance but not crudely linked to output, as with Taylor, but measured by a number of specific objectives such as customer satisfaction or delivery. It has become much more prominent in the public sector and associated with the ideas of New Public Management, which involves instilling private sector discipline. In addition, it has become ubiquitous, even in countries where other models of pay were more embedded, such as seniority pay in Japan. It is an interesting question as to if and how performance-related pay should be implemented in cultures with very different values from the Western world, especially those that are more collectivist and oriented to the team or group.

Much of the reason for the spread of its popularity relates to the persuasiveness of the term itself, like other Anglo/American concepts such as high-performance work systems (see Chapter 3)—who could be opposed to something apparently so commonsensical as performance-related pay? What then explains the limited evidence as to its positive impact? One issue is expectation: performance-related pay creates a sense of entitlement; 'if I do well and work hard, I should get more money'. If more money is not forthcoming, then it could be demotivating. Human nature is also a factor in these expectations: there is the 'Lake Wobegon effect' (an illusory superiority complex) when people perceive their performance to be above average (as drivers, lovers, spouses, and workers) and are consequently disappointed if they do not get the expected return.

Others suggest that any successes may be less to do with motivation effects of the opportunity to meet goals and get more money but more the performance management dimension side: staff value being given opportunities for personal development, goal setting, and talking about their job with a mentor and this is what leads to behaviour change, not the prospect of more money.

There are also issues of how the performance assessment is judged and the myriad of biases that can creep in. In a study by Stephen

Scullen and colleagues, idiosyncratic rater effects (an individual rater's peculiarities of perception) accounted for more than half of the rating variance, with actual performance accounting for only 21 per cent of the variance. Thus, what performance assessment measures is not so much the performance of the ratee, but the unique rating tendencies of the rater; in short, ratings can reveal more about the rater than they do about the ratee.

The evaluation of performance is a central part of HRM with performance evaluated as part of a broader review and the functioning of the whole organization. Performance management should link together strategy, performance objectives, and standards by measuring and developing individuals, and performance appraisal (PA) is part of this process. PA has many purposes including evaluation, succession planning, development, motivation, and auditing, and these multiple possible uses create problems, as they may conflict. If, for example, PA is about evaluation (and might include bonuses), then the individual may be tempted to hide deficiencies. If it is primarily to do with development, then areas for improvement are exactly what need to be discussed. PA is frequently described as being a conversation, but a conversation about development places us in a very different mental place from where one is being judged and rated. If there is ranking and grading this interferes with the development process and encourages people to work at how to look good rather than how to get better. The focus becomes the rating and, given this, staff are unlikely to openly discuss performance problems. Furthermore, reviews for ratings tend to be backward-looking, and future development needs may be overlooked. The unintended consequence of having ratings is that staff become obsessed with achieving good ratings, supervisors get nervous about how their rating will be received, and the notion of development drops out of the conversation, which is where the real value is. Many systems no longer have the confidence of key stakeholders with reviews seen as bureaucratic, expensive, time-consuming, and irksome exercises carried out to satisfy the HR function. Ironically, the process is often based on some other person wanting it: appraisees do it for their supervisors, who do it for their managers, who do it for HR, who themselves are not that enthusiastic about it. The main purpose is often to have completed it, with success being measured by everyone completing a process rather than delivering value to staff and managers, which is rarely assessed. It is rather telling that some organizations say they are in fact more likely to take action against employees for not filling in the forms than for poor performance itself.

As we have noted throughout, the practice of day-to-day HRM is not with HR or senior managers, but implemented by line managers, and PA is no different. These managers need to retain relationships with their staff, and so perhaps not surprisingly there is an element of grade inflation. One can see their point: when a person has slaved all year at Workingyouhard.com and they then find that their performance is satisfactory (aka average), it does not instil much warm feeling or commitment towards the manager or the organization. So, ratings tend to be compressed and consequently higher. In response, organizations have used forced ranking systems so that a certain percentage can be fitted into each category. Some notoriously have a 'rank or yank' system, made popular (in the press, not among those to whom it was applied) by General Electric under Jack Welch and practised also by Enron. Here they rank employees along a normal distribution curve in which the top 10 per cent typically receive an A grade, the middle 80 per cent earn a B, and the bottom 10 per cent earn a C and dismissal if they do not improve.

In response to the problems discussed, many high-profile companies such as General Electric, Microsoft, Google, Netflix, Adobe, and Accenture have dropped traditional annual evaluations, as they are seen as being unfit for purpose in terms of helping and driving performance. Deloitte famously claimed that their PM system with meetings, forms, and ratings cost them two million hours each year and one exhaustive review concluded that 'formal PM processes disengage employees, cost millions, and have no impact on performance'.

There are also many cultural issues to do with evaluation. In France, managers felt they had no control over the objective set (contrary to goal-setting ideas) and hence saw the process as more like entrapment and were at best sceptical about the idea of a two-way conversation with managers and employees. In countries such as China, evaluation can be personally threatening and loss of face affects an individual's reputation so stakes can be high.

Although the jury is out on some aspects of performance evaluation, many organizations have moved away from set-piece annual reviews to more regular and informal check-ins.

Executive pay and associated packages such as bonuses and stock options have been headline news in recent years. A major concern has been the gap between the highest and the lowest paid, which has accelerated over the last 30 years. The High Pay Centre in the UK presented data that FTSE 100 CEOs earn 117 times more than the average UK worker (getting the typical worker's annual salary in about 33 hours) and found scant evidence to justify such a huge gap. There are variations across the globe. CEOs of large firms in Japan earn only 10 per cent of equivalent American ones and 20 per cent of those in the UK. To provide some comparison over time, in 1963 the CEO ratio of pay to staff was 20, by 1978 it was 30, by 1991 121, and by 2019 it was 278. Does this motivate chief executives to work harder? One might think the first few million might be enough to get the full attention and focus of the CEO, and they might not need bonuses to do the job they have been paid for, but according to personnel economic theory, high pay is not about creating motivation for the CEO but more about motivating everyone further down the chain to attempt to attain that job. Partly as a result of disquiet in this area, we are now seeing in the UK remuneration committees in large organizations

Halos, horns, cronies, and doppelgängers

A halo effect is where one positive criterion distorts the assessment of others.

The horns effect is where a single negative aspect dominates the rating.

The doppelgänger effect is where the rating reflects the similarity between appraiser and appraised.

The crony effect is the result of the appraisal being distorted by the closeness of the relationship between appraiser and appraised.

The Veblen effect is named after the economist who gave all his students a C-grade irrespective of the quality of their work. Thus, all those appraised received middle-order ratings.

The impression effect is the problem of distinguishing actual performance from calculated 'impression management'. The impression management tactics of employees can result in supervisors liking them more and thus rating their job performance more highly. Employees often attempt to manage their reputations by substituting measures of process (effort, behaviour, etc.) for measures of outcome (results), particularly when the results are less than favourable.

being responsible for setting executive pay and overseeing fair pay more generally, and there will be further scrutiny given to the need to report pay ratios. There is a danger that current pay systems with huge pay gaps across the corporate ladder attribute economic value to a dominant executive group with value creation couched in terms of the contribution of heroic individuals rather than broader distributed leadership and organizational contribution. This is a wider concern than simply affecting individual businesses as it impacts wealth distribution and societal equalities. Across most market economies, for example, there has been an unprecedented widening pay gap, coupled with more people living in poverty, including those in paid employment ('in-work poverty'). Furthermore, with the decline in collective bargaining to provide checks and balances to excessive executive remuneration, HRM can exercise an ethical role. At the very least HR could ensure accurate payment given that the role of inspection is very limited, such that, as David Metcalf (the former director of Labour Market Enforcement in the UK) pointed out, companies could expect a minimum wage inspection on average once every 500 years.

A long-standing issue is that of gender pay equity. According to the World Economic Forum, the global pay gap between women and men will take 202 years to close. In the UK the gender pay gap is around 14 per cent. From an earlier focus of legislation examining different pay for doing the same job, the scope is now wider and if a woman is doing work of the same value as a man, even if it is a different job, she can claim equal pay. The move to publish pay gaps will help make companies' compliance transparent. In 2017 the BBC was forced to publish the salaries of TV stars earning £150,000 and higher, and this exposed that men were paid much more than their female counterparts. Meanwhile in the USA, Google, with over 20,000 staff and an annual income of $28 billion, complained of the burden of obtaining wage data to the US Department of Labor in relation to a government audit. According to a recent Chartered Institute of Personnel and Development report in the UK, 60 per cent of all organizations have gender pay gap reports although not all share the findings with employees. Although 60 per cent of organizations stated that they talk about the fairness of pay processes and outcomes, only 10 per cent of staff said that their line manager did this with them.

The gender pay gap is persistent: why is this? Damian Grimshaw and Jill Rubery, Employment Scholars in the UK, point out that women's skills are less visible in pay structures or skill classifications compared to those of men. Traditional men's occupations are classified and rewarded according to much more fine-grained divisions between type and degree of skill compared to much of women's work, which tends to be aggregated together, as with retail or care work. Vocation can be used to legitimize low pay, on the grounds that as women derive considerable satisfaction from their work (more altruistic) they need less compensation. In addition, women are underrepresented in sectors where the cost of labour is a low proportion of costs and where employers thus have perhaps more scope to pay higher wages without this damaging competitiveness. They are more often employed in areas such as retail or the care industry. And there is what they term variance: that women do not always fit with the traditional norms, such as long working hours. There is often a premium in certain jobs for working more than 50 hours per week, especially in professional and managerial occupations, which raises men's wages relative to women's, who, because they bear the bulk of childcare responsibilities, are not always able to match the working hours of men. The recent pandemic has highlighted the fact that much of the work where females dominate is actually the essential work that keeps society ticking: teaching, retail, nursing, cleaning, childcare. While many white-collar workers can actually stay at home, society still functions because of the work of others who are the essential workers.

Moreover, part-time workers (who are more often women than men) have to negotiate specific arrangements with their employers and hence have limited bargaining power. Unfortunately, improvements to women's pay in the public sector, where the scale of the employer has a major impact on women's pay, have also been undermined by outsourcing and centralized wage freezes or caps on pay below inflation. And flexibility in contracts has been a mixed blessing as employers focus on increasing productivity through cutting out less productive hours such as when customer demand is low. This has led to greater work intensity and irregularity in shift patterns such as split shifts, fragmented work arrangements, and periods of underemployment.

A good example illustrating where gender bias can be built into systems can be seen in a case about firefighters in New York City. In 1981 the city had a physical abilities test, which included candidates wearing full firefighting gear and hauling a bag of concrete on their shoulders up six flights of stairs. Many women and some men could not pass this test, and this led to a legal case. As part of this case Wayne Cascio looked at what these firefighters actually did and found that firefighters never put people over their shoulders and ran up stairs. Most of the time they are running down the stairs, and in smoke they were trained to stay as low to the ground as possible. In short, the test was not related to the actual job. Some 20 years later, Brenda Berkman (who brought the original case to court) was one of the heroes of 9/11, running up 60 flights of stairs in the North Tower to rescue people.

In all this, much of the literature in the field tends to be prescriptive, that is we are told how management should tackle reward and indeed how employees should react, but not always what actually happens in practice. The reader needs to reflect on the other benefits of work: the reward package is somewhat more than the payment system alone, incorporating a range of financial and non-financial benefits. What are the rewards of going to work? Beyond wages, bonuses, and pensions, it provides friends, community, meaning, satisfaction, and HRM needs to move beyond the idea that pay is the only answer. HRM also needs to address issues of fairness and equity in pursuit of the humanization of the workplace.

Chapter 5
Having a say at work

When to speak up and when to stay silent? This is the subject of studies on employee voice and is an issue we face daily. In recent years, many organizational disasters, for example the Space Shuttle *Challenger*, the collapse of Enron, United Airlines 173 crash, the 'Dr Death' case in an Australian hospital, and the Rana Plaza disaster (the collapse of the garments factory in Dhaka, Bangladesh), could have been averted if there had been effective employee voice. In other words, what if an organization had information regarding problems, but did not access it or did not act based on this information? Mathew Syed's book *Black Box Thinking* presents two powerful stories, one from aviation and the other from health, illustrating the consequences of failed voice. Both these cases had deadly consequences, despite the relevant information to avert disaster being in the room or cockpit where the decisions were being made. In the first instance, the co-pilot had alerted the pilot that the plane was soon to run out of fuel, but did not raise the matter again as he felt that the pilot had received the warning and would not welcome further interruption as he sought to get the wheels down so as to land the plane. In the second, during anaesthesia for a routine operation, an otherwise healthy 37-year-old went from going under to inoperably brain damaged in 20 minutes, despite two anaesthetists and a surgeon retrying their methods to feed oxygen to the airways. At 12 minutes a nurse suggested a standard life-saving procedure and had the equipment available for use. But with the experts fixated on only one solution, the nurse felt too junior to further interrupt, expecting that they knew better.

So speaking up to save lives is important, as is speaking up with ideas and suggestions to help improve organizational functioning and employee interests. In short, employee voice concerns the ways and means through which employees attempt to have a say and potentially influence organizational affairs about issues that affect their work and the interests of the organization. This can involve a variety of voice mechanisms: for instance formal and informal, direct and indirect, union and non-union. It encompasses individual employee behaviours such as suggestions to help management but also includes the ways in which employees might challenge managerial behaviour, such as raising issues to do with inequity or inadequate safety. Voice has both cooperative and conflictual aspects. The notion of increasing levels of employee voice to influence work activities and organizational decision-making is not new. In the early 20th century, Hugo Munsterberg's *Psychology and Industrial Efficiency* (1913), William Basset's *When the Workmen Help you Manage* (1919), and Elton Mayo's *The Human Problems of an Industrial Civilization* (the Hawthorne studies) from the mid-1930s are examples of the long interest in employee voice.

The workplace is where people spend much of their lives doing things under the direction of others. At the same time employers are paying for both brain and brawn: the employees are there to work and follow reasonable instruction to help the employer with their goals, whether it be better customer service or more widgets. In this context voice is valuable to workers as it allows them to express views and make suggestions and in doing so contributes to their dignity—not slaves following orders but workers whose views are respected. Given this, workers need a voice and managers need to provide them with an opportunity to speak and encouragement to do so. So far so good: but many workplaces remain modelled on the 'manager knows best' or, as the Russian saying goes, 'I'm the boss, you're the fool', and top-down autocratic styles based on management from a hundred years ago. These models still exist today, as one manager told me in an interview: 'Why do I need to think Joe from stores has anything to offer me, if he did, he would not be Joe from stores.' It is a crushing and depressing view of how managers view their staff. While the saying is that 'With every pair of hands, you get a free brain', we are not always using the brain.

The model of scientific management established by Taylor and then operationalized in car assembly lines has been significant in management thinking. Reflecting this attitude, Henry Ford complained that 'When I want a pair of hands I get a human being as well.' Taylor's ideal worker was not an all-rounder: 'One of the very first requirements for a man who is fit to handle pig iron as a regular occupation is that he shall be so stupid and phlegmatic that he more nearly resembles in his mental make up the ox.' Taylorism, and the notion that brains should only be used by managers with other workers simply following orders, has cast a long shadow over management approaches.

One way of approaching these issues is to consider that from an organizational perspective heavily prescribed work with little discretion might be seen as requiring little voice, whereas work which allows for high levels of discretion requires a lot more. Much of the business impetus behind employee voice came in the late 1980s and was associated with related initiatives such as empowerment and involvement. Such ideas were advocated by the influential popular management writers/gurus of this period, including Tom Peters and Richard Schonberger, whose ideas popularized giving workers greater say. Peters's advice was to 'involve everyone in everything; leading by empowering people', and Schonberger commented that 'we want take charge employees', exhorting organizations to give employees greater control. The new management paradigm emphasized by writers such as Peter Drucker and Rosabeth Moss Kanter embraces concepts such as de-bureaucratization (end of hierarchy and prescriptive rules), delayering, decentralization, and the utilization of project-based teams as part of a movement towards a new knowledge-based organization. The new approach carried implications for management as compliance—hierarchical authority was to be replaced by high-trust relations, teamwork, and voice. More recently, employee engagement has continued this approach with a much-cited Watson Wyatt study demonstrating that a company with highly engaged employees achieves a financial performance four times better than those with poor engagement. The attraction of employee engagement is that it can be everything to everybody. In recent years, the sweet smell of its novelty may have soured, given one survey found half of workers would prefer to fill in an online shopping survey than an engagement survey. But for genuine engagement, voice is critical. In other words, engagement is not just about getting workers to listen better to managers (top down) but having a dialogue that involves worker voice.

There is a terrible irony in that managers spend a lot of time discussing the war for talent, but then can fail to take much interest in the talent that is available to them. Employee voice is central to this, making the most of resources that are available to managers, but too easily treated as an inconvenience. Ironically, workers are enthusiastic, energetic, and creative *except* when they are at work. In fact, many years ago, a study pointed out that people used more skill driving to work in the morning than they used at work.

Progressive employers see voice as valuable, as workers are on the front line and have access to critical information which does not always get to the top (new ideas facilitate continuous improvement, as with the Japanese Kaizen movement). With many jobs being more complex than in the days of scientific management, giving employees discretion to provide better

Long lunch: Spanish civil servant skips work for years without anyone noticing

Joaquín García failed to show up for his job at the water board for at least six years - and possibly as many as 14

4. Jon Henley, 'Long lunch', *The Guardian*, 13 February 2016.

service and achieve a higher standard of work makes sense. Thus, voice can help problem-solving, creates a climate for innovation, and serves as an alert to potential problems. The critical information is often in the organization, but does not get out, or if it gets out, does not get to the right people, or if it gets to the right people, they fail to act. This is a question of 'voice systems', which we will return to later.

Notions of engagement include such things as being enthusiastic and passionate about the job and connecting with work colleagues and organizational goals, but in actual fact this is relatively rare if we look around us. The example of the Spanish civil servant who went missing for up to 14 years—while being paid—is fortunately not typical but is a form of extreme disengagement (Figure 4). According to the *Guardian* newspaper, it was only when Joaquín García was due to collect an award for long service at the water board that anyone realized that he had not, in fact, shown up to work for at least six years. Garcia was fined €27,000 (£21,000) by the court, which had earlier found that the engineer did not appear to have occupied his office for 'at least six years' and had done 'absolutely no work' between 2007 and 2010, the years before he retired. García told the court that he had turned up to the office but kept irregular hours. He also claimed he was the victim of workplace bullying and was sidelined because of his family's politics. It appeared that the water board had believed García was the responsibility of the city council while the city council thought he was working for the water board. García did not spend his time idly, but apparently became an expert on the Dutch philosopher Spinoza.

That people should have a say in matters that concern them and affect their working lives seems to be indisputable and, as noted above, they should clearly speak up when there are problems that should be brought to the attention of managers. Indeed, managers and employees should both have an interest in speaking up. Why, then, can voice be so contentious in the workplace? Part of the answer is that voice is embedded in the employment relationship and needs to be seen in that context. Voice is part of the 'frontier of control' in the workplace. But this frontier is not static but contested and is shaped by the interaction of both management and employees in furthering their respective interests.

Voice is not just about business benefits, and the ability to have a say is a human right linked to the concept of industrial citizenship (or industrial democracy). Here, voice is seen as a fundamental democratic right for workers, a means of extending a degree of control over managerial decision-making in an organization. While there are a number of popular books which talk about democracy at work, on closer inspection they are more about making people feel part of a team culture with everyone working together. The idea that workers might use voice to express interests that are separate from, and sometimes in conflict with, those of management is not usually part of the picture.

When we are looking at voice that pushes back against management prerogative we cannot isolate the exercise of voice from its institutional context: factors such as labour law or unionization will have an effect on speaking up as well as individual traits that would lead some employees to 'choose' voice, while others 'choose' to remain silent.

It is also important to look at voice in a comparative context—it is very easy to see the local perspective as the universal perspective or take the US model as the norm. However, once we widen our lens, we see that in many European countries, for instance, the state plays a much more active role. France has Statutory Elected Workers' Councils, while Germany has co-determination based on Works Councils and Worker Directors. Without statutory provisions for employee voice, more is left to the preferences of managers to establish their own arrangements, and indeed the purpose of these bodies may differ by country, for instance to deliver business benefits or to allow for other voices and agendas to be heard. Countries with high 'power-distance' cultures, that is those with more acceptance of hierarchy and unequal power relations, are less likely to be receptive to employee voice.

Of course, a democratic but bankrupt organization is no good to anyone, nor are cumbersome decision-making systems. As Oscar Wilde said about socialism, 'the trouble was it involved too many evenings…'. Consultation can slow decision-making and potentially narrow the range of decision options for management. In some contexts, too much voice and democracy might not be helpful. In the military, officers expect orders to be obeyed, and obeyed quickly, without the need for consensus on whether storming the machine-gun post is a good idea. But even in the military, front-line ideas and observations could provide vital information to those behind the lines making the strategy. Indeed, following orders may not always be good in a crisis. As noted earlier in relation to the United Airlines 173 accident, the plane ran out of fuel while the pilot was focused on getting the undercarriage down. In the review, which led to a new approach to training around a Crew Resource Management approach, the inability of the crew to work and communicate with one another effectively was identified as a key factor in the accident. Research shows that crew often do not speak up as they fear damaging relationships or being punished. Some people have suggested that culture is a major factor: deferential cultures create barriers as there is an unequal power relationship in the cockpit, and it is felt that a subordinate should not question the decisions or actions of superiors.

In relation to airline accident rates, collectivist national cultures have about three times more accidents per capita than do individualistic national cultures, and high power-distance nations have about 2½ times more accidents per capita than do low power-distance nations. One explanation is that there is less openness and questioning in collectivist and high power-distance cultures. In a study on introducing quality circles (problem-solving work groups) in Singapore, it was clear that workers are hesitant to make known their views about work problems because they deem themselves unqualified to do so, and because they fear that they may offend or 'show up' their co-workers. The problem of 'kiasuism'—or the fear of losing face—also impeded Singapore workers from participating voluntarily in these bottom-up improvement activities. Workers felt that by bringing up their work problems, they were highlighting their own deficiencies to their managers and co-workers, or they feared that their suggestions were not good enough and that they might be shown up by better ideas from others.

A central issue in relation to employee voice is management prerogative. The classic 'voice' model that Albert Hirschman wrote about in *Exit, Voice, and Loyalty* (1970) suggested that when facing dissatisfaction the options were to exit (i.e. to withdraw from the relationship) *or* to voice (i.e. to speak up to seek improvements). While his work was carried out in relation to consumer goods, the ideas were extended into a number of contexts including that of the employment relationship.

Indeed, this is evident in small firms where voice options are limited, or the owner is the only voice avenue and also (often) the source of the problem. If people raise their voices to be shot down as troublemakers, as not being team players, as too focused on problems, or as being pessimistic, then this does not encourage the others. A staff member on the Prime Minister Theresa May's disastrous 2017 election campaign pointed out: 'bringing bad news was treated as unhelpful, disloyal, not "Team May"—the behaviour if you spoke up was just so bad, you shut up'. Here, silence is likely to be the best option for employees if sanction, retaliation, or career limitation are the likely outcomes. The Samuel Goldwyn story that *I don't want yes-men around me. I want everyone to tell me the truth—even though it costs him his job* is not likely to encourage voice.

A nice illustration of the context of not speaking up can be seen in the famous study by sociologist Robert Jackall:

> (1) You never go around your boss. (2) You tell your boss what he wants to hear, even when your boss claims that he wants dissenting views. (3) If your boss wants something dropped, you drop it. (4) You are sensitive to your boss's wishes so that you anticipate what he wants: you don't force him, in other words, to act as boss. (5) Your job is not to report something that your boss does not want reported, but rather to cover it up. You do what your job requires, and keep your mouth shut.

But while most research suggests that employees want the opportunity to have a say and contribute to the work issues that matter to them, to what extent do they get this? Most organizations above a certain size have some structures for voice, but the way voice initiatives actually work may depend on whether they are perceived as authentic. That is, are managers actually interested in hearing their employees' voices, and will they do something about their concerns or suggestions? Too often, voice becomes spitting in the wind, which has little impact and leads to workers becoming demoralized as management pays little attention to resolving issues. While there is often a focus by managers on establishing voice systems, there also needs to be active listening and response to what these voice systems feed back to them.

First, a voice system is set up by the organization to shape and channel voice. The system has a number of dimensions including the degree, level, range, and scope of issues that are within the purview of the voice system. The degree indicates the extent to which employees are able to influence decisions about various aspects of management—are they simply informed of changes, consulted, or actually involved in making decisions? One organization talked of the new wave of voice as moving from telling people what to do, to telling them why they were being instructed what to do. This is very different from the ideal in which workers are empowered and take decisions on pay and holidays.

Second, there is the level at which voice is expressed, in other words, where the voicing takes place. Is it at the work-group level or department or even corporate level? This is important because some issues are better dealt with at specific levels, so voice must reach that level to have influence. The range of subject matter is the third aspect of voice: from housekeeping—such as canteen food—to more strategic concerns, relating to investment strategies, for example.

Lastly, there is the form that voice takes, which could include workers making decisions as part of their daily job responsibilities, as opposed to workers making suggestions through a formal scheme. This is not to say the voice system operates as designed by managers, but that the system describes the intent of designers of the system. A voice system has both institutional and human elements, that is, both structure and agency.

But what is the purpose of the voice system? Here, expectations might be different. Managers tend to see voice as synonymous with terms such as 'consultation', 'communication', and 'say'. What is notable in the study of management attitudes to voice is the tendency to view it as more about the transmission of information than as a dialogue. Grievance procedures are frequently not regarded as an expression of voice by management. So, managers can see voice as providing a lubrication of the management system but may not be so keen on allowing voice which fundamentally challenges the system. Therefore, the issue becomes that of who controls the agenda for voice (and silence). In some instances, voice has been interpreted by managers as employees listening better to managers! Hence, employee voice can sometimes be interpreted simply as *manager's* voice, and this relates to the interest in recent years in management increasing downward communication to employees, to 'win hearts and minds'. This is then designed not to provide 'better' information to empower workers, but to convince them of the logic of management decisions that are actual or impending.

There are benefits in terms of genuine collaboration with employers, unions, and workers. In the United States, it has been observed that workplace innovation, especially when it has occurred in unionized establishments, is positively associated with labour productivity. These authors inferred that this strong effect in unionized workplaces could be the result of workers being more willing to participate in employee involvement programmes and voice if they feel the union will protect their employment security. The US healthcare company Kaiser Permanente took a partnership approach to addressing problems and showed what could be achieved with a high-trust collaborative approach with staff and the unions. This helped turn around Kaiser Permanente's financial performance, built and sustained a record of labour peace, and demonstrated the value of partnership in negotiating national labour agreements and resolving problems on a day-to-day basis.

Of course, this highlights an important point: managers need legitimacy. They prefer to operate with the support of employees, so part of voice is to consult even if managers prefer endorsement rather than feedback. This is tricky for managers, however, and is a good illustration of people management as a craft rather than the application of rules or standards. Simply put, if asking workers for their views never really changes anything, people may not bother to contribute and legitimacy erodes. To get something, management must give something away, even if it is a crumb or two to show it is worth getting involved. But creating voice structures also creates expectations, and while management may wish voice to be defined around certain specific issues, their ability to limit voice to these issues cannot be taken for granted. Equally, if the intention of management is to create a weak voice structure, then it can be seen by workers as a body with no credibility that, paradoxically, may well encourage workers to look outside for someone more independent to represent their views or vent through social media. It may well be that the appetite for voice might ebb and flow, as we found in looking at voice over a 25-year period in a financial services organization where collaboration collapsed under the pressure of the Global Financial Crisis but then was the subject of a concerted attempt to rebuild systems and trust in its aftermath.

Why do people speak up? We have all been to meetings where the call for questions is met by silence. Some might say that speaking up can be explained by individual characteristics (e.g. confidence and an outgoing nature), and this may provide part of the answer. But there are also system issues. Management, through agenda-setting, can perpetuate silence over a range of issues, in effect, organizing them out of the voice process. In other words, if you attend a meeting and the item you thought was on the table is not there, this makes it more difficult to discuss. Management may want to open up some things, but keep others closed; they may want some discussion of how things might be done differently, but not necessarily discussion on what things should be done in the first place. Worker absence and turnover might be on the table but not managers' pay. Leadership matters in the operation of voice: one CEO at the Alocoa aluminium plant in the USA wanted to bring down accident rates and gave his phone number to workers so if they were concerned they could call him. He found that they did call him but often with many other interesting ideas. This also points to the importance of having multiple channels of voice available.

Of course, silence is not always bad for management; there are whole areas of organizational life where silence is expedient for management and where it may often be in their interest in the maintenance of the status quo. Employee voice mechanisms are often defined according to management's own interpretations of what the expression of voice is taken to mean, thus shaping the prevailing climate in an organization and the extent of influence which employees feel they have over matters that affect them. Work done by Tony Royle shows how McDonald's in Germany was able to shape (manipulate) the existing system of co-determination by narrowing the scope of the Company Works Council to issues exclusively of managerial concern, like customer service and quality, rather than worker-focused issues.

A good example of how voice systems can fail can be seen in the Dr Death case at Bundaberg Base Hospital (BBH) in regional Australia, where a doctor was alleged to have caused at least 18 deaths through negligence. Medical staff making mistakes is not a new phenomenon, but this was a rare case where employees attempted to voice concerns and a substantial system failure led to very public and extended legal proceedings that opened internal processes to scrutiny. In fact, the doctor had received, during his time at the hospital, no fewer than 20 complaints against him relating to incompetence, unnecessary surgery, performing surgery above his skills, and hygiene concerns. But these complaints were not acted upon by management (complaints which broke through the hierarchy were often downplayed or ignored). In fact, the doctor won employee of the month even while this was happening.

According to a director of medicine, BBH had a history of a 'pleasing the boss' culture, and complaints were often not forwarded or were reworded to appear less negative. The nurse who became the eventual whistle blower had attempted to use internal avenues, including meeting with the Director of Nursing, writing detailed complaints, and finally approaching the local Member of Parliament. So, here is a testbed of voice: the hospital had multiple, well-established voice channels and staff were professionally trained and motivated. The problem was that the messages that were transmitted through the voice system appeared not to be taken seriously. One thing that became apparent was that some voices were more valued than others. So it was harder for a nurse to suggest fault with a doctor's clinical judgement than to complete a form for a faulty piece of equipment. Management was clearly disinclined to pursue complaints voiced due to the potential impact on funding and publicity, and employees were warned of their obligations under the Code of Conduct and that speaking to outside sources could have serious ramifications for their job security. Yet speaking up can save lives. Reports in the health sector suggest large numbers of preventable errors, with one famous study indicating 400,000 premature deaths associated with preventable harm, including the wrong drugs being administered or operating on the wrong part of the body. Making preventable errors is the third largest killer in the USA behind heart disease and cancer, but ahead of guns and motor vehicle accidents.

Table 3. Ten ways to stifle voice

Reprisals: kill the messenger
Deaf ear syndrome
Kicking into the long grass
I know best
Only tell me good news
Tell someone who cares
Bring me solutions
Trickle up voice
SEP (someone else's problem)
Please do not reply

But voice is difficult to do well: it is not cost free and middle managers at the heart of day-to-day employee voice can feel threatened by the changes in the role and style that often accompany notions of voice. It is not surprising that they do not universally welcome it. Consultation sessions can be seen as a 'necessary evil' to be endured, or as 'joint aggravation sessions' (as they were once described to me). So, when we encourage voice, we need to remember that it is easier to give orders and sometimes easier to just follow them. Table 3 illustrates the ways that voice can be muted as a result of managerial messages that can intentionally or unintentionally stifle voice. Reprisals tend to kill off voice directly. Ignoring voice (deaf ear syndrome) or delaying responses (the long grass) also stifle voice, as does a manager who is always the expert on everything. Other responses tend to mute voice indirectly. Asking for only good news or solutions signals that it is not always a good idea to bring up problems. Equally, suggesting that it is not for them to take an interest in a particular issue (someone else's problem), or not taking responsibility to pass voice on but assuming it will find a way to trickle up, are other ways of limiting voice. The 'please do not reply' automatic email sends a message that we do not want to hear your views and offers no suggestion of where to provide feedback.

How does free speech link to voice? This came up in the row over the Google engineer who was fired after circulating a memo suggesting women lacked the skills for a career in technology, or the case of Israel Folau, the Australian rugby player who had his contract torn up after posting on his website that 'those that are living in sin will end up in Hell unless you repent', helpfully adding his target audience of 'drunks, homosexuals, adulterers, liars, fornicators, thieves, atheists and idolaters'. So while speaking up in a work context is generally seen as something to be encouraged, free speech within a work context must be balanced against other considerations.

Employee voice might be seen as a sure-fire route to the re-enchantment of work. If we recognize conflicts, then voice is about dialogue and resolution. Voice is not just about benefiting the organization, but also a means of correcting unfairness or mistreatment, challenging management, or indeed as a vehicle for employee self-determination and an expression of an individual's exercise of personal control over the collective. So, it is not surprising that we have voice gaps in the workplace.

There are competing expectations of 'employee voice'. While voice has important democratic implications, given a choice, managers tend only to be interested if there is a perceived pay-off. That might be the avoidance of issues or trouble because of the early warning system or it could represent a more positive role. However, for voice to have legitimacy it needs to be about more than the managerial concept of efficiency and adding value to business.

As we have seen, employee voice does place higher expectations on managers. Although the CEO or the Human Resource Function may give strategic direction and profess enthusiasm for the notion of voice, it is at the line-manager level that voice is enacted. Line managers may frustrate, lubricate, or bypass voice opportunities because of their lack of confidence, belief, or training. So, these managers need to be developed and trained with support for this new role; moving from policing (catching people doing things wrong) to coaching (supporting and developing staff).

Traditional voice practices, such as face-to-face bargaining, consultation, or involvement, are now being supplemented or replaced with social media and modern communication technology as forms of voice. This might indicate that modern generations of workers will not be as easily silenced, as modes of voice that are not controlled by management are available for workers to vent.

And people do have more formal channels at work, for example Yammer and Teams. However, it is also worth noting that these official channels are often monitored so people may prefer to communicate on their own devices, such as private WhatsApp chats. We also observe the blur between work and home freedom of speech with Facebook, Twitter, etc. social media policies. When the Cambodian garment sector was in crisis during the Covid pandemic with clothing orders cancelled, government guidance not to sack the workers but reduce pay and send them home was ignored. A worker posting their factory's plans to fire workers on Facebook was arrested and faced criminal charges for inciting unrest and fake news.

Organizations are increasingly likely to face a diffuse but persistent range of concerns from highly articulate employees. We should remind ourselves that however management try to control voice, they are not all-powerful. Today, social media means employees or ex-employees can damage corporate reputations swiftly and shutting down voices in one forum can mean they simply migrate elsewhere. Others argue that when employees do not speak up, this can be a type of protest in the form of active employee silence. In some contexts, remaining silent can carry as much or more of a message as speaking up. This is the 'thunder in silence' in the Chinese sage Lao-tzu's philosophy about how to voice discontent. But while 'getting-back' or protesting employer actions by actively not offering ideas may carry the message of discontent, it does not offer the mechanism for finding solutions. Voice is central to rehumanizing the workplace.

Chapter 6
Saying goodbye?
Downsizing—are human
resources assets or liabilities?

Much HRM literature focuses on mapping a virtuous pathway to
nirvana (a combination of business performance and happy
workers), and texts are heavy on talent management. The focus is
on an onward and upwards representation of organizations and
their relationship with staff (the team). HRM managers recruit;
train; devise strategies; manage rewards, talent, and careers;
engage employees; and solve problems for the mutual benefit of
the organization (and workforce), and in doing so create excellent,
world class, leading organizations. The general tone is upbeat,
even evangelical; to reach for the stars with change (a term more
commonly used by managers than restructuring), and actions are
framed as a positive process of 'rooting out inertia', promoting
efficiency, focusing on core competencies, and fostering
innovation. Take a look at the airport bookshelves next time you
are there. How much homespun optimism can you see glowing?
But what Gibson Burrell dubbed 'Heathrow organisation theory'
is bereft of books on downsizing...

Indeed, if we go to the library and look at the row of HRM texts,
we will find very limited coverage of downsizing. It is not only
HRM books but change and strategy books which give downsizing
a wide berth, although the focus on core competencies and

reducing overheads hints at a relationship. It is interesting to note downsizing is rather more in evidence in the Dilbert cartoons by Scott Adams and in films (e.g. *Up in the Air*, *Roger and Me*, and *The Full Monty*) than it is in HRM texts. Reactions to downsizing do make the news, from strikes to factory occupations and 'bossnappings'.

This is really the dark side of organizational life; but how the process is handled can tell us a great deal about HRM in the organization as it is lived rather than merely espoused. As individuals or organizations we reveal our true values when under pressure. The mission statements and branding may be very eloquent in showcasing the espoused values and how the organization would like to be seen, but crisis reveals the true values and preferences of organizations. Are buildings valued more than people? Is satisfying shareholders more valued than retaining staff? Is HRM then really about developing people or helping balance the books?

Organizations are continually expanding, contracting, and restructuring, with jobs often being affected. Downsizing is a fact of business life and by extension therefore of HRM, and is something that is widely practised. The Global Financial Crisis (GFC) witnessed 8.5 million lay-offs in the USA and 25 million laid off from state-owned firms in China, and the Covid-19 crisis at the time of writing has led to 3 million unemployed in the UK with over 9 million covered by the furlough scheme of state subsidies for jobs. The pandemic has seen 93 per cent of the world's workers residing in nations with unprecedented workplace closures, as well as working-hour losses four times greater than during the financial crisis in 2009, and over 100 million job losses reported in 2020 (ILO, 2020). So we see the role of the state as an important actor affecting downsizing with furloughed wage subsidy schemes around Covid in many countries. This is more equitable than the situation in the wake of the GFC in 2008, when governments bailed out banks for 'being too big to fail', yet many other jobs were not saved. So choices matter here, and the state as an external actor is key, including support (or lack of it) for industry and workers, as well as setting the stage for what is good practice, including consultation laws.

But while it is commonplace or unremarkable as a brute fact, existing coverage of downsizing tends to be around legal requirements in dealing with the process rather than how to avoid it or how to effect it in the least painful way. Although there is more research available today, the why, how, and when of making people redundant needs to be explored further. Given the emphasis on change management in HRM, it is perhaps a strange omission, especially given the negative consequences it often has. We know that those downsized can suffer from financial hardship, decline in mental well-being, and social and relationship strain. These issues were put into dramatic effect in *The Full Monty*, a 1997 film set in Sheffield, the British city famous for its steel-making industry. The film shows the impact of redundancy on a group of steelworkers. The manager, humiliated by what had happened, was unable even to discuss his redundancy with his wife and pretended to go to work every morning, briefcase in hand, with his wife only learning the truth when the bailiffs came to the house after he had failed to pay the bills. One study reported that individuals who had experienced even a single financial, job-related, or housing impact during the recession in the USA in 2008 still had higher odds of symptoms of depression, generalized anxiety, panic, and problematic substance use some three to four years after the recession had ended.

One proposition advanced by scholars to explain this absence of attention is the 'mafia model' of downsizing. In this model, downsizing is best seen as an anomalous (and rather unpleasant) component of HRM, best hurriedly carried out without public viewing, not discussed, and then forgotten. It is often timed before Christmas or the summer holidays, so there is a psychological break as people are 'disappeared'. However, whether looking at the

UK, the USA, or elsewhere in the world, it appears that downsizing is not a once and for all event at all. And indeed, cutting salary costs to improve organizational performance is popular with management, and is a major part of the strategic armoury in turning around troubled organizations. A drop in costs shows on the bottom line quickly and indicates to shareholders that the management means business (or are a mean business). Downsizing can be seen as a sign of corporate virility as managers take tough decisions. For instance, Barclays Bank shares were reported as soaring in 1999 after its announcement to axe 6,000 staff. But work by Wayne Cascio shows that those who absorb more pain and delay the downsizing process do better two years later, so the quick fix approach may not actually work. Part of the issue is that in many cases people are hired back later and consultants are brought in to replace others who left and there may be retraining needed. This, together with lower morale, can exhaust the organization and have a negative effect on culture, identification, commitment, and innovation (who wants to take risks now?), reducing its ability to be flexible and agile. Indeed, one study found there was an adverse association with all the employee outcomes investigated (e.g. inability to detach, energy depletion, anxiety, work attitudes) and most of the work conditions (e.g. work role, interpersonal aspects, rewards, and security).

Downsizing is a broad concept that can encompass various combinations of reductions in company assets—financial, physical, or human—but our focus is of course employment, and this is about lay-offs and redundancies, not to be confused with 'downscoping', which concerns divestiture of assets and businesses that are unrelated to the organization's core business. Downsizing is the planned elimination of jobs. Downsizing and restructuring are often used interchangeably (the latter can be used as a euphemism by managers although most workers see it as bad news), but organizations can of course restructure without reducing staff and vice versa.

The aim of downsizing is usually set out as a long list, including labour-cost savings, faster decision-making, improved communication, reduced product development time, enhanced involvement of employees, and greater responsiveness to customers. Michael Hammer, for example, argued that cutting positions and management hierarchies leads to a flat organization with an empowered multi-skilled workforce, which encourages innovation.

But given that in the era of a knowledge-based economy, competitive advantage depends very much on human assets, intellectual capital, and the ability to use tacit knowledge, a stable work environment is important. Robert Cole argues that employee turnover damages organizational memory insofar as individual organizational members are 'a primary repository of an organization's operational knowledge and trust' that cannot easily be replaced, as it is impossible to document. A concern is that organizations intending to become lean and mean, instead end up 'lean and lame' or even anorexic. So, mismanagement in this area of HRM can be damaging for both organizational reputation and impact on staff, whether they are staying or leaving. One interesting aspect of this is how the terms used by managers for downsizing tend to be euphemistic (Table 4).

Other colourful terms include 'increasing the velocity of organizational exit' as if people were being fired from a cannon or 'liberating from our organization those who could not fit in', which makes it sound as if they were the enemy who needed routing. The international bank HSBC got into the news with its announcement that it was 'demising' over 1,000 staff despite profits of over £13 billion. It is worth reflecting that worker discourse by contrast is very blunt: they are being sacked, fired, or axed.

The attempt by organizations to distance themselves from what might be seen as dirty work can be seen in the movie *Up in the*

Table 4. Sacked, demised, or pursuing new opportunities?

a career alternative enhancement programme
career reappraisal
compressing
de-cluttering
de-recruiting
de-hiring
de-jobbing
demising
disemploying
headcount reduction
involuntary quit
letting-go
non-retaining
payroll adjustment
Previously Unrecognized Recruitment Errors
rebalancing
resizing
rightsizing
shedding
slimming
streamlining
surplused
synergy related headcount adjustment
unassigned
volume-related production schedule adjustment

Air, starring George Clooney as a consultant who works for a firm that specializes in 'termination assistance'. Clooney's character, Ryan, travels the country firing people on behalf of employers and building up air miles. When a new employee suggests a more efficient process using videoconferencing, Ryan complains it is too impersonal, and after a trial run that ends in the suicide of one of those in receipt of the news, the face-to-face model is reinstated and our hero can return to 30,000 feet. At least our hero did not have to deal with the deputies and supervisors fired by a newly elected sheriff at Clayton County, Georgia. On this occasion, staff who thought they were being invited to a swearing-in ceremony had their badges, guns, and car keys removed, and were then fired and escorted to a police van to take them home, while being overseen by rooftop snipers who were there 'just in case someone got emotional'.

At other times even when the downsizing process is not de-personalized it can seem insensitive. Walmart in the USA laid off workers, notifying them two hours ahead of time, and provided them with a packet of information offering stress management tips to cope with the job loss, including avoiding caffeine, chocolate, nicotine, and alcohol. In addition, they encouraged workers to get professional counselling and said that 'difficulty sleeping, nightmares, flashbacks and feelings of being hyper-alert are common and will diminish over time' (Figure 5).

Managers often use metaphors to frame the strategy, and in relation to the practice of downsizing the dominant metaphor is 'lean'. Organizations are encouraged to be lean and agile as opposed to being flabby or bloated. Indeed, as Melissa Tyler and I explored, the metaphor conceals the pursuit of a 'thin' ideal in contemporary organizational life more generally (the tyranny of slenderness). We noted that the contention is that managerial discourses on downsizing dehumanize people, who are represented as 'corporate fat'. If you can never be too rich or too thin, so it seems equally that corporations can never be too profitable nor too lean. In short, downsizing is about the pursuit of a fit and healthy (organizational) body which represents the organization as disciplined, dynamic, and agile. Yahoo announced plans to become *more fit* by reducing staff by 10 per cent and Tesla

5. Jobseekers in the Depression.

claimed its redundancies were akin to a special forces' philosophy. Equally, legal frameworks can facilitate organizational fat trimming—contract workers, temps, agency workers can be shed quickly, as the law permits, just as if by taking a magic diet pill.

It is a truth but not universally acknowledged that many organizations, whether in the public or private sectors across the European, Australasian, and US economies, have a preoccupation with cost-cutting, so seek to reduce staff numbers on a yearly basis. There are variations in the appetite for staff cuts; among those in the more liberal market economies there is rather more willingness to treat employees as commodity costs—it is simply an accepted business recipe in pursuit of being lean and is facilitated by laws as well as custom and practice.

However, there is a concern that the cost-cutting regime associated with many organizational change strategies has fractured the traditional employment relationships, so that some writers advocate the notion of human resource sustainability to deal with concerns over staff turnover, loyalty, and stress. HRM has an important role to play in all of this, preferably being involved upstream as decisions are taken, rather than being reduced to the deliverers of bad news or organizing the delivery of bad news. It should be no surprise that research confirms that downsizing is more likely to be effective over the longer term when it goes hand in hand with HR practices such as communication, respectful treatment of redundant employees, and attention to survivors' concerns. Equally, post-downsizing HR practices are needed to promote the discretionary efforts of employees, retain valuable human capital, and reconstruct valuable organization structures, as the negative effects can spill over onto those left who suffer from 'survivor syndrome', which incorporates declining motivation, reduced capacity for change, decline in loyalty to the organization, and psychological withdrawal as workers can feel embittered towards management, anxious about their future, and guilty about still having a job. One study found that the response of survivors is closely linked to the treatment received by those laid off so HR is important here. Sadly, as Peter Cappelli points out, senior HR specialists were not involved in lay-off decisions during the GFC in two-thirds of organizations.

As we might expect, the impact of downsizing on the organization and staff is very much affected by the way it is implemented. Some organizations deploy a big-bang approach, with the activity being carried out within a tight time-frame, whereas others take a more gradual approach. At one end of the spectrum, organizations can be seen as reactive, while at the other they are seen as more pro-active. One study reported that 94 per cent of human resource managers had less than two months to plan and implement downsizing within their organization, which clearly inhibits strategic planning. Kim Cameron famously described the big-bang approach as akin to 'throwing a grenade into a crowded room, closing the door, and expecting the explosion to eliminate a certain percentage of the workforce. It is difficult to predict exactly who will be eliminated and who will remain.' Clearly this approach increases the likelihood of arbitrary action, given the haste to get people out, and can mean simply getting rid of those who are easiest to remove rather than keeping the right people. If management feels able to take a longer time to implement downsizing, there may be more opportunity for better communication and indeed allowing employees to provide their perspective, input, and suggestions. Consultation with employees increases the likelihood of some commitment or at least acceptance of decisions being made, which helps with implementation.

As Kim Cameron suggests there are three main approaches to downsizing as set out in Table 5.

It is no surprise to find that, in addition to speed, the magnitude of downsizing exacerbates its impact. And if we take a social capital perspective, it is likely that major reductions in staff will damage trust, organizational memory, and networks, which all reduce performance outcomes.

A recent concern is that downsizing is no longer the preserve of the desperate or sick, but increasingly of financially healthy companies who want to boost earnings. The celebrated CEO Jack Welch was known as 'neutron Jack' for his penchant for firing staff but leaving the buildings intact, with 10,000 jobs going in five years. Also operating in the USA was 'Chainsaw' Al Dunlap, who got rid of 11,000 staff in two months, which represented over a third of the workforce. One possible explanation for this approach is that rising income inequality between CEOs and ordinary workers creates extreme power asymmetries in the workplace, and these power differences lead to CEOs behaving in a selfish fashion toward those workers further down the ranks who they cannot really identify with.

Table 5. Three types of downsizing strategy

	Workforce reduction	Work redesign	Systemic
Focus	Headcount	Jobs, levels, units	Culture
Eliminate	People	Work	Status quo
Implementation time	Quick	Moderate	Extended
Pay-off target	Short-term pay-off	Moderate-term pay-off	Long-term pay-off
Inhibits	Long-term adaptability	Quick payback	Short-term cost savings
Examples	Attrition Lay-offs Early retirement Buy-out packages	Combine functions Merge units Redesign jobs Eliminate layers	Involve everyone Simplify everything Bottom-up change Target hidden costs

As we see stakeholder orientation being eroded by shareholder values and a move from a managerial model of business to a shareholder or financial model of the firm, organizations increasingly make money from a range of financial activities that have very little to do with producing goods or services, for example mergers and acquisitions. They are selling off assets and other financial products to enhance profits. Famously, GM made more money through its credit card arm than from selling cars. This has been referred to as financialization.

Are there alternatives to explore first? Is downsizing the only viable tool for managers to wield? Organizations do have strategic choices in the face of demand shortfalls. There are, in fact, an array of possible approaches, with significant differences across countries. In the USA, with employment at will and a 'hire and fire' philosophy, workers tend to be shed both more quickly and at a higher rate than in European countries, where there is rather more emphasis on finding alternatives. Partly, this relates to the regulatory framework, with the role of the state more embedded in social and employment policy. In Germany, there is *Kurzarbeit*, 'short work', which allows firms to temporarily reduce working time in a downturn to reduce labour costs, while a proportion of the shortfall for employees is made up by the government in the form of a short-time working payment. The companies pay only for the hours worked, while the government provides up to 67 per cent of the workers' remaining wages, resulting in saving half a million jobs in the GFC. In France there is the *chômage partiel* (partial unemployment) scheme. In countries such as Japan, graded steps for cost reduction are built into operations, such as redeployment, relocation, retraining, transfer, and even suspending dividend pay-outs and cutting the salaries of senior managers. Indeed, Japan has historically had lifetime employment as one of its main pillars, locking in loyalty to the corporation, although this has been under pressure for some years as businesses seek more flexibility and some Japanese corporations have developed 'Career Redesign Rooms', also known as 'chasing out rooms', where employees who refuse to take early retirement are allocated rooms with menial work on which they have to file reports in the hope they might then be shamed into leaving.

Wayne Cascio talks about the different mental models that senior managers have in relation to the people working being costs to be cut or assets to be developed:

> The downsizers see employees as commodities—like paper clips or light bulbs, interchangeable and substitutable for one another. This is a 'plug in' mentality: plug them in when you need them; pull the plug when you no longer need them. In contrast, responsible

restructurers see employees as sources of innovation and renewal. They see in employees the potential to grow their businesses.

Wage cuts as an alternative to job cuts tend to be sparingly used. Thomas Cook Travel agents in 2001 cut 1,500 jobs and staff took pay cuts of up to 10 per cent, as business collapsed after the 9/11 attacks. Flexible working arrangements have also been used, as when automotive companies including Honda, Nissan, and BMW reduced working time at their plants. Redeployment is another part of the toolkit, although sometimes done in a rather macho manner: a European automobile equipment multinational, Continental, sent a letter to 600 out of 1,120 dismissed staff, offering job relocations to Tunisia for salaries of €137 a month and argued that this complied with the legal obligation to relocate staff in existing operations within the company. These issues were also much debated during the early years of the Great Depression (and more recently in the Covid crisis of 2020, where the term 'furlough' entered the public vocabulary).

These approaches facilitate a rapid expansion when normality returns. It is interesting to observe that during the GFC in the UK, most employers favoured alternative measures to job losses where possible. There are optimistic and pessimistic perspectives on why this was the case. Does this mean employers had learnt that downsizing is bad and were pursuing more responsible approaches to reducing costs, or perhaps had already cut back down so severely that there was no fat to trim? Or had they shifted towards more flexible work models, for example agency, contract for services, etc.?

Seventy-five per cent made at least one employment-related change in response to the recession, and some of the most widely used included freezing and cutting pay (41 per cent), freezing recruitment (28 per cent), reorganizing work (25 per cent), as well as reducing overtime (19 per cent), use of agency staff (15 per cent), and reduced working hours (14 per cent). Ten per cent of organizations made compulsory redundancies and 7 per cent voluntary redundancies. In the Covid-19 crisis, two-thirds of UK employers furloughed workers using the government's job retention scheme to avoid making redundancies.

In terms of adjusting the workforce but without compulsory redundancy, how do we get to what the Koreans term 'honourable retirement'? A favoured approach is called natural wastage, where people are not replaced as they leave the organization. Voluntary redundancy is another option, although there are issues regarding expense, as employees with long service find it attractive, and also the best workers who can get jobs elsewhere are more likely to leave. Offering early retirement with sweetened packages is another possibility, although it is often seen more as a method of avoiding downsizing.

If there is no other option and downsizing does take place, consultation with employees is critical. 'Cornflake redundancy' was the name given to those redundancies when workers found out they had lost their jobs while eating breakfast (and usually from reading the paper), and this led to changes in EU regulation. Too often secrecy is the watchword, with managers insisting on their prerogative to hire and fire staff and close down businesses, and considering consultation a distraction. But there are examples of unions and management working together during a consultation period to identify alternative cost savings in the budget, as in the case of a financial services organization in the UK who used their partnership approach to find common ground and save jobs. In any process, what is critical is a sense of fairness and organizational justice. Workers need a voice in the process and also to feel that the selection process was fair and is not being used to weed out 'troublemakers'.

We learn a lot about HRM and organizational values as practised rather than simply espoused, by looking at how organizations treat staff in difficult circumstances: who they decide should let you know your services are not required, whether it is done by a stranger, by HR, or in person by your manager; whether it is done face to face, by email, by video, or (as we saw sometimes happens) by reading it in the newspaper.

The tension between the 'Human Resources' and the 'Management' in HRM is very much to the fore in the downsizing process. There is clearly a role for HR beyond the procedural aspects of redundancy, such as fairness around selection, getting more involved and earlier in the strategic aspects of decision-making, championing its most important asset (people), as well as encouraging senior managers to act in line with pronounced organizational values. Indeed, Bill Roche and Paul Teague found that HR have gained influence in decision-making in many organizations during the recession as they were dependent on HR expertise in implementing retrenchment programmes, but that their role was limited to developing and implementing short-term reactive measures to keep businesses afloat and did not extend to becoming more influential or strategically embedded as the organization moved out of crisis. However, while this might seem disappointing, it was noteworthy that HR did not simply apply a set of technical practices but were guided by shared values about the appropriate actions to follow in crisis, including the importance of communication, of treating employees fairly, with dignity and respect, and of managers acting with probity and honesty.

Chapter 7
Conclusion

As this book was being completed the world was in the grip of the Covid-19 pandemic, a public health and global economic crisis that presented challenges well beyond the scope of HRM. States responded to this crisis in varying ways. For example, the UK and USA delayed their social isolation measures, and unemployment support mechanisms were variable and difficult to navigate due to fears of disrupting free market values. New Zealand and some other continental European countries, on the other hand, stepped in to support workers and businesses more quickly and announced lockdowns very early in the pandemic, with a strong set of regulations. Responses also varied at the organizational level, and here HRM as an academic subject and the HR function were both front and centre during the pandemic. We have seen downsizing, staff cuts, and business closures with trade ceasing alongside other more employee-friendly approaches, such as (partial) continued wage payments, hiring freezes, flexible arrangements (working remotely and variable hours), and reduced spending on non-salary functions.

All the HRM issues discussed in this book were given a fresh twist by workers not going in to work during the pandemic, raising a host of questions. What is the workplace? How do workers voice without being at work? How do you reward and motivate employees? How can well-being be managed? How is the workplace culture to be maintained? HRM experts have had to grapple with all of this and come up with solutions fast. But it is not simply a new twist on HRM that we have seen. To some extent the crisis has laid bare trends that were already under way in our society and shone a light on the implications of these trends. For instance, we found workers outside the world of mainstream HRM such as the self-employed (not covered by HRM at all) through to those who are more peripheral to the main HRM stage—those on contract, part-time workers, casual workers, and other precarious workers—being poorly catered for in terms of support. It also showed large divergences between essential workers of low market value yet high value to society such as cleaners and delivery drivers.

Covid-19 may accelerate the restructuring of the way work is performed, especially with the use of technologies in those industries that were not previously impacted by digitalization. And while new technologies can be a beneficial part of re-humanizing work by allowing for the flexibility of home working, they can also be invasive and used for surveillance and control.

It is also important to note that while much popular literature sees a context in which universal forces are unleashed upon the world of work (as if there was no human agency), research indicates that there is considerable unevenness in the workplace, and institutional arrangements at the national level have a major impact on how broad trends play out. Thus, the old model of HRM is being eroded: long-tenure jobs with good pay and benefits, and a psychological contract based on a quid pro quo of employee loyalty for job security, is being displaced by a more market-mediated relationship including shorter-term jobs with multiple employers and a shift of employment risk to employees.

But societies and organizations can make choices: in France a move to limit emails out of hours was one attempt, the so-called *right to disconnect*; South Korea, with long working hours but low

6. L. S. Lowry, *Going to Work*.

engagement, rewarded supervisors not just on output but how early their staff can go home; and Volkswagen shut off mobile communications for several days at a time. These might seem modest shifts in the nature of management but they are at least attempts to marry well-being and performance to develop a quality of working life agenda to support worker well-being (Figure 6).

So, what can HRM practitioners do to make work less dehumanizing? Can we design better systems and practices that produce good outcomes for employers and employees that combine profitability and well-being, where workers do not regard work as a grind, but somewhere they can fulfil their potential and be respected? At the very least, can we create environments where the worst time of the week is not when workers are with their boss. Perhaps less focus on wellness programmes and yoga and more on the management practices that lead to reduced well-being are needed. Equally, we do not want to overlook the collective aspects of employment and the contested terrain in which management choices are made. Nor is it just a matter of good and bad managers and how to improve our managerial capability, but of how an overall strategy can be configured to consider the value of workers so that such considerations are built into the business model. So, taking the high road to HRM rather than a low-cost, sweat-the-people approach means having a strategy that incorporates well-trained and innovative employees who can add value to the organization. This sets the platform for a more ambitious HRM approach which makes use of worker talents. And importantly it is making the most of all worker talent, not simply lavishing attention and resources on a select group. Equality, diversity, and fairness are vital to a functioning workplace. Nor is this about extracting the greatest shareholder value at the expense of the workers. HR needs to engage with all stakeholders, not just shareholders and senior executives.

In Australia there was an illuminating story of discovered talents in the context of the Covid pandemic. A commercial laundry, which employed a large number of migrant workers, faced a significant downturn in business. It turned to its workers to see what else they could offer and discovered that the company's 25 migrant workers had 31 university degrees between them. Their qualifications were in areas where the company needed help (in IT and quality assurance). Workers were promoted into these roles rather than management looking externally for these human resources.

HRM should be about making the most of human talent and creating value as well as ensuring that workers share in the outcomes of value creation, not just shareholders. The aim of mutual gains is a possible and worthwhile goal. And we need to have longer-term sustainable contributions based on values such as fairness. For better or worse, Covid-19 has shone a light on HRM in all our organizations. This is not to say that customers, profit, or shareholders are irrelevant—without customers and profit, there are no jobs; it is about ensuring that *both* are considered. HRM should be part of a strategy for longer-term business development with a pluralist perspective with a wider range of stakeholders considered, and looking at longer-term business sustainability, rather than a quick fix. HRM is concerned with not just strategy but employee welfare and has a strong ethical responsibility which needs to be incorporated into day-to-day decisions.

In many respects we want more of what the HRM literature talks about: workers with talents being utilized for the benefit of employers and workers. The realities of work with precarity and in-work poverty seem at odds with the promise of HRM. More positive or humanizing approaches depend not just on employers but also corporate governance and actors at national level.

Management need to think of the talents of their employees and how to utilize them rather taking a controlling approach which can contribute to the very things to be feared and avoided: as Sumitra Ghoshal has noted, the use of surveillance, monitoring, and authority leads management to distrust employees and, in a vicious circle, to the perceived need for even more surveillance and control.

> Because all behaviour is seen by managers as motivated by the controls in place, they develop a jaundiced view of their people. For the employees, the use of hierarchal controls signals that they are neither trusted nor trustworthy to behave appropriately without such controls...One of the likely consequences of eroding attitudes is a shift from consummate and voluntary cooperation to perfunctory compliance.

This might explain why 'presenteeism' is still an idea with value: like the Hollywood film mogul who needed to hear typing to know his screenwriters were working, Yahoo hit the news by restricting working remotely, and workers at the *Telegraph* newspaper found heat and motion sensors tracking their movements without their knowledge, ostensibly to ensure optimal usage of space. But have we now moved into a new arena with working at home becoming the norm during the Covid crisis? Organizations are reporting higher productivity in this context, so this might mean managers are able to rethink their mental models of work (and workers) to allow for a higher-trust approach. But there are also those organizations that are using the technology to monitor workers, such as being active on Microsoft Teams or Slack, with employees who do not have them on or are not active on them being seen as absent from work or not working. Similarly, the financial services firm PwC developed a facial recognition tool that logged when employees working at home were absent from their computer screens, and these employees were reportedly requested to provide a written reason for their absence, including going to the bathroom. One might note pessimistically that even at the height of the crisis (at least in the UK), employers were nagging staff to get back to the office to 'look visible' even when they could work adequately from home, which suggests that management attitudes remain suspicious of homeworking and that presenteeism is alive and strong!

So while the pandemic has accelerated trends that were on the horizon anyway (homeworking, tech use), is this a temporary disruption or will the legacy be a more significant transformation? Working hard? Or hardly working? It is a tragedy that lives are wasted in hours of work where there is little meaning or dignity, despite being surrounded by so many people with skills and talents who have effectively checked out and disengaged from their day-to-day work or quit in their seat. As a report from a consulting firm (CEB's Global Talent Monitor) showed, only 22 per cent of staff were showing high discretionary efforts. Ethical and equitable Human Resource practices can re-humanize work by being pluralistic and inclusive. People spend a great proportion of their waking lives at work and HRM can help make those working lives worth living.

References and further reading

Chapter 1: What is Human Resource Management and why does it matter?

Bryson, A., and Mackerron, G. (2017), 'Are you happy while you work?', *The Economic Journal*, 127(599), 106–25.

Pollard, S. (1965), *The Genesis of Modern Management: A Study of the Industrial Revolution in Great Britain*, Edward Arnold, London.

Bowden, B., and McMurray, A. (eds) (2020), *The Palgrave Handbook of Management History*, Palgrave Macmillan, Cheltenham.

Wilkinson, A., Armstrong, S., and Lounsbury, M. (eds) (2017), *The Oxford Handbook of Management*, Oxford University Press, Oxford.

Landes, D. (1983), *Revolution in Time: Clocks and the Making of the Modern World*, Belknap Press of Harvard University Press, Boston.

Willman, P. (2014), *Understanding Management*, Cambridge University Press, Cambridge.

Gospel, H. (2019), 'Human resource management: a historical perspective', in Wilkinson, A., Bacon, N., Lepak, D., and Snell, S. (eds), *The Sage Handbook of Human Resource Management* (2nd edition), Sage, London.

Drucker, P. (1954), *The Practice of Management*, Harper Row, New York, p. 238.

Sisson, K. (2010), *Employment Relations Matters*, University of Warwick, Coventry.

Discussions in this chapter and the book as a whole have also been informed by books including: Wilkinson, A., Bacon, N., Snell, S., and Lepak, D. (2019), *The Sage Handbook of Human Resource*

Management (2nd edition), Sage, London; Wilkinson, A., Dundon, T., and Redman, T. (eds), *Contemporary Human Resource Management* (6th edition), Sage, London; Marchington, M., Wilkinson, A., Donnelly, R., and Knogiou, A. (2020), *Human Resource Management at Work* (7th edition), CIPD, London. Ulrich, D. (1997), *Human Resource Champions: The Next Agenda for Adding Value and Delivering Results*, Harvard Business School Press, Boston; and Torrington, D., Hall, L., Taylor, S., and Atkinson, C. (2017), *Human Resource Management* (9th edition), FT Prentice Hall, London.

Chapter 2: HRM: strategy and performance

Drucker, P. (1961), *The Practice of Management*, Mercury, London, pp. 269–70, quoted in Legge, K. (1995), *Human Resource Management: Rhetorics and Realities*, Macmillan, Basingstoke, p. 6.

Walton, R. A. (1985), 'From control to commitment in the workplace', *Harvard Business Review*, 63(2), 77–84, p. 77.

Beer, M., Spector, B., Lawrence, P., Mills, Q., and Walton, R. (1984), *Managing Human Assets*, The Free Press, New York, pp. 49–61.

Fombrun, C., Tichy, N., and Devanna, M. (1984), *Strategic Human Resource Management*, Wiley, New York.

Powell, T. C. (2017), 'Strategy as diligence: putting behavioral strategy into practice', *California Management Review*, 59(3), 162–90.

Sull, D., Sull, C., and Yoder, J. (2018), 'No one knows your strategy—not even your top leaders', *MIT Sloan Management Review* (Summer), 1–11.

Huselid, M. A. (1995), 'The impact of human resource management practices on turnover, productivity, and corporate financial performance', *Academy of Management Journal*, 38, 635–72.

Ichniowski, C., Kochan, T., Levine, D., Olson, O., and Strauss, G. (1996), 'What works at work', *Industrial Relations*, 35(3), 299–333.

Appelbaum, E., Bailey, T., Berg, P., and Kalleberg, A. (2000), *Manufacturing Competitive Advantage: The Effects of High Performance Work Systems on Plant Performance and Company Outcomes*, Cornell University Press, New York.

Pfeffer, P. (1998), *The Human Equation*, Harvard Business School Press, Boston.

Purcell, J. (1999), 'Best practice and best fit: chimera or cul-de-sac?', *Human Resource Management Journal*, 9(3), 26–41, p. 36.

Barney, J. (1995), 'Looking inside for competitive advantage', *Academy of Management Executive*, 9(4), 49–61.

Mueller, F. (1996), 'Human resources as strategic assets: an evolutionary resource-based theory', *Journal of Management Studies*, 33(6), 757–85.

Boxall, P. (2018), 'The development of strategic HRM: reflections on a 30-year journey', *Labour & Industry: A Journal of the Social and Economic Relations of Work*, 28(1), 21–30.

Boxall, P. (2012), 'High-performance work systems: what, why, how and for whom?', *Asia Pacific Journal of Human Resources*, 50, 169–86.

Godard, J. (2020), 'Labor and employment practices: the rise and fall of the new managerialism', in Bowden, B., and McMurray, A. (eds), *The Palgrave Handbook of Management History*, Palgrave Macmillan, Cheltenham.

Kaufman, B. E. (2020), 'The real problem: the deadly combination of psychologisation, scientism, and normative promotionalism takes strategic human resource management down a 30-year dead end', *Human Resource Management Journal*, 30, 49–72.

Chapter 3: Who does HRM and how?

Lee, Q., Townsend, K., and Wilkinson, A. (2020), 'Frontline managers' implementation of the formal and informal performance management systems', *Personnel Review*, DOI 10.1108/PR-11-2019-0639.

Whyte, W. (1960), *The Organization Man*, Simon & Schuster, New York.

Redman, T., Wilkinson, A., and Snape, E. (1997), 'Stuck in the middle? Managers in building societies', *Work, Employment and Society*, 11(1), 101–14.

Schein, E. (1986), *Organisational Culture and Leadership*, Jossey Bass, Hoboken, NJ.

Townsend, K., Wilkinson, A., Bamber, G., and Allan, C. (2012), 'Accidental, unprepared, and unsupported: clinical nurses becoming managers', *The International Journal of Human Resource Management*, 23(1), 204–20.

Wilkinson, A., Marchington, M., Goodman, J., and Ackers, P. (1993), 'Refashioning industrial relations: the experience of a chemical company over the last decade', *Personnel Review*, 22(2), 22–38.

Purcell, J., and Kinnie, N. (2007). 'HRM and business performance', in Boxall, P. F., Purcell, J., and Wright, P. (eds), *The Oxford Handbook of Human Resource Management*. Oxford University Press, pp. 533–51.

Woodrow, C., and Guest, D. (2014), 'When good HR gets bad results: exploring the challenge of HR implementation in the case of workplace bullying', *Human Resource Management Journal*, 24(1), 38–56.

Ackroyd, S., and Crowdy, P. (1990), 'Can culture be managed? Working with "raw" material: the case of the English slaughter-men', *Personnel Review*, 19(5), 3–13.

Hamper, B. (1991), *Rivethead: Tales from the Assembly Line*, Warner Books, New York.

Grugulis, I., and Wilkinson, A. (2002), 'Managing culture at British Airways: hype, hope and reality', *Long Range Planning*, 35(2), 179–94.

Wood, A. (2020), *Despotism on Demand: How Power Operates in the Flexible Workplace*, Cornell University Press, Ithaca, NY.

Wilkinson, A., Barry, M., Kaufman, B., and Gomez, R. (2018), *Taking the Pulse at Work: Employer–Employee Relations and Workplace Problems in Australia Compared to the United States*, Centre for Work, Organisation and Wellbeing, Griffith University, Brisbane.

Wilkinson, A., Barry, M., Gomez, R., and Kaufman, B. E. (2018), 'Taking the pulse at work: an employment relations scorecard for Australia', *Journal of Industrial Relations*, 60(2), 145–75.

Chapter 4: Managing performance and rewards

Lawler, E. (1995), 'The new pay: a strategic approach', *Compensation & Benefits Review*, 27(4), 14–22.

World at Work (2015), *The World at Work Handbook of Compensation, Benefits and Total Rewards*, John Wiley & Sons, Chichester.

MacRae, I., and Furnham, A. (2017), *Motivation and Performance: A Guide to Motivating a Diverse Workforce*, Kogan Page, London.

Kerr, S. (1995), 'On the folly of rewarding A, while hoping for B', *The Academy of Management Executive*, 9(1), 7–14.

Bryson, A., and MacKerron, G. (2017), 'Are you happy while you work?', *The Economic Journal*, 127(599), 106–25.

Whyte, W. (1955), *Money and Motivation: An Analysis of Incentives in Industry*, Harpur, New York.

Donkin, R. (2001), *Blood, Sweat and Tears: The Evolution of Work*, Texere Publishing, New York.

Roy, D. (1952), 'Quota restriction and goldbricking in a machine shop', *American Journal of Sociology*, 57, 478–85.

Maslow, A. (1954), *Motivation and Personality*, Harper & Row, New York.

Schein, E. (1988), *Organizational Psychology*, Prentice Hall, New Jersey.

Herzberg, F. (1968), *Work and the Nature of Man*, Staples Press, London.

Kohn, A. (2018), *Punished by Rewards: The Trouble with Gold Stars, Incentive Plans, A's, Praise, and Other Bribes*, Houghton Mifflin, Boston.

Pink, D. (2009), *Drive*, Riverhead Books, NY.

Rock, D., Davis, J., and Jones, B. (2014), 'Kill your performance ratings', *strategy+business*, 76.

Sharot, T. (2017), 'What motivates employees more: rewards or punishments?', *Harvard Business Review* (May), <https://hbr.org/2017/09/what-motivates-employees-more-rewards-or-punishments>.

Whyte, S. (2020), "Great Instagram moment': McCormack says Australians should pick fruit for photo ops', *The Canberra Times*, September.

Ferguson, A. (2018), 'Dollarmites bites: the scandal behind the Commonwealth Bank's junior savings program', *Sydney Morning Herald*, May.

Lazear, E. (1995), *Personnel Economics*, MIT Press, London.

Janofsky, M. (1993), 'Domino's ends fast-pizza pledge after big award to crash victim', *New York Times*, 22 December.

Parkinson, H. (2019), 'Parcel in the toilet: why you should never blame the delivery driver', *Guardian*, 28 March 2019.

Orsini, J. N. (1987), 'Bonuses: what is the impact?', *National Productivity Review*, 6(2), 180–4.

BBC (2013), 'Police fix crime statistics to meet targets, MPs told BBC', 19 November.

Smith, A. (1776), *An Inquiry into the Nature and Causes of the Wealth of Nations*, par. I.2.2.

Crace, J. (2019), 'Stockpiles of despair at record levels after another week of Brexit', *Guardian*, 1 February.

Kruger, J., and Dunning, D. (1999), 'Unskilled and unaware of it: how difficulties in recognizing one's own incompetence lead to inflated self-assessments', *Journal of Personality and Social Psychology*, 77, 1121–34.

Scullen, S. E., Mount, M. K., and Goff, M. (2000), 'Understanding the latent structure of job performance ratings', *Journal of Applied Psychology*, 85(6), 54–60.

Buckingham, M., and Goodall, A. (2015), 'Reinventing performance management', *Harvard Business Review*, April 2015 issue, viewed 5 May 2020, <https://hbr.org/2015/04/reinventing-performance-management>.

Deming, W. E. (1986), *Out of the Crisis*, MIT Press, London.

Pulakos, E., Mueller-Hanson, R., and Arad, S. (2019), 'The evolution of performance management: searching for value', *Annual Review of Organizational Psychology and Organizational Behavior*, 6(1), 249–71.

Redman, T. (2001), 'Performance appraisal', in Redman, T., and Wilkinson, A. (eds), *Contemporary Human Resource Management*, Pearson, London.

Treo, G. (1973), 'Management style a la française', *European Business* (Autumn), 71–9.

CIPD (2020), 'Top bosses' pay overtakes average worker's entire 2020 pay in just 3 days', https://www.cipd.co.uk/about/media/press/high-pay-day-2020#gref.

O'Connor, S. (2019), 'A minimum wage is pointless if we don't enforce it', *Prospect Magazine*, 30 January.

CIPD, 'Gender pay gap reporting | Topic page | CIPD', https://www.cipd.co.uk/about/who-we-are/cipd-pay-gap-reports/gender#gref.

Grimshaw, D., and Rubery, J. (2007), 'Undervaluing women's work', Equal Opportunities Commission Manchester, Working Paper Series No. 53. http://www.equalityhumanrights.com/uploaded_files/equalpay/undervaluing_womens_work.pdf.

Hebson, G., and Rubery, J. (2018), 'Employment relations and gender equality', in Wilkinson, A., Dundon, T., Donaghey, J., and Colvin, A. (eds), *The Routledge Companion to Employment Relations*, Abingdon, Routledge, pp. 93–107.

Goldin, C. (2017), 'How to win the battle of the sexes over pay (hint: it isn't simple)', *The New York Times*, 10 November 2017, viewed 5 May 2020, <https://www.nytimes.com/2017/11/10/business/how-to-win-the-battle-of-the-sexes-over-pay-.html>.

Cha, Y., and Weeden, K. (2014), 'Overwork and the slow convergence in the gender gap in wages', *American Sociological Review*, 79(3), 457–84.

AHRI (2012), 'An interview with Professor Wayne Cascio', 27 June 2012, hrmonline.com.au.

Martínez Lucio, M., and McBride, J. (2020), 'Recognising the value and significance of cleaning work in a context of crisis', <http://blog.policy.manchester.ac.uk/posts/2020/06/recognising-the-value-and-significance-of-cleaning-work-in-a-context-of-crisis>.

Chapter 5: Having a say at work

Syed, M. (2016), *Black Box Thinking*, John Murray Press, London.

Munsterberg, H. (1913), *Psychology and Industrial Efficiency*, Houghton Mifflin Co., Boston.

Basset, W. (1919), *When the Workmen Help you Manage*, Century Co., New York.

Mayo, E. (1933), *The Human Problems of an Industrial Civilization*, Arno Press, New York.

Kaufman, B. (2020), 'Employee voice before Hirschman: its early history, conceptualization and practice', in Wilkinson, A., et al. (eds), *Handbook of Employee Voice* (2nd edition), Edward Elgar, Cheltenham, pp. 17–35.

Peters, T. (1989), *Thriving on Chaos: Handbook for a Management Revolution*, Knopf Publishing, New York.

Schonberger, R. (1990), *Building a Chain of Customers: Linking Business Function to Create a World-Class Company*, The Free Press, New York.

Kanter, R. (1989), 'The new managerial work', *Harvard Business Review*, 66, 85–92.

Semler, R. (1993), *Maverick! The Success Story Behind the World's Most Unusual Workplace*, Warner Books, New York.

Wyatt, W. (2009), *Continuous Engagement: The Key to Unlocking the Value of Your People During Tough Times, Work Europe Survey 2008–2009*, London.

Clark, L. (2016), 'Why a new pair of jeans may be more compelling than employee engagement', *Blessing White eNews* (May), viewed 1 June 2020, <https://blessingwhite.com/new-pair-jeans-may-compelling-employee-engagement/>.

Blackburn, R., and Mann, M. (1979), *The Working Class in the Labour Market*, Palgrave Macmillan, London.

Henley, J. (2016), 'Long lunch: Spanish civil servant skips work for years without anyone noticing', *Guardian*, 13 February, viewed 1 June 2020, <https://www.theguardian.com/world/2016/feb/12/long-lunch-spanish-civil-servant-skips-work-for-years-without-anyone-noticing>.

Goodrich, C. (1975), *The Frontier of Control*, Pluto Press, New York.

Barry, M., and Wilkinson, A. (2016), 'Pro-social or pro-management? A critique of the conception of employee voice as a pro-social behaviour within organizational behaviour', *British Journal of Industrial Relations*, 54, 261–84.

Philips, D. (1994), 'Culture may play a role in flight safety', *Washington Post*, 22 August, viewed 1 June 2020, <https://archive.seattletimes.com/archive/?date=19940822&slug=1926593>.

Yong, J., and Wilkinson, A. (1999), 'The state of total quality management: a review', *The International Journal of Human Resource Management*, 10(1), 137–61.

Hirschman, A. (1970), *Exit, Voice, and Loyalty: Responses to Decline in Firms, Organizations, and States*, Harvard University Press, Cambridge.

Hinsliff, G. (2017), 'Theresa May won't survive long. Tory modernisers are already plotting', *Guardian*, 10 June 2017.

Alvesson, M., and Spicer, A. (2012), 'A stupidity-based theory of organizations', *Journal of Management Studies*, 49(7), 1194–220.

Jackall, R. (1988), *Moral Mazes: The World of Corporate Managers & Mazes*, Oxford University Press, New York, pp. 109–10.

Black, S., and Lynch, L. (2004), 'What's driving the new economy? The benefits of workplace innovation', *The Economic Journal*, 114(493), F97–F116.

Kochan, T. (2016), 'The Kaiser Permanente labour–management partnership: 1997–2013', in Johnstone, S., and Wilkinson, A. (eds), *Developing Positive Employment Relations*, Palgrave Macmillan, London, pp. 249–80.

Johnstone, S., and Wilkinson, A. (2018), 'The potential of labour–management partnership: a longitudinal case analysis', *British Journal of Management*, 29, 554–70.

Donaghey, J., Cullinane, N., Dundon, T., and Wilkinson, A. (2011), 'Reconceptualising employee silence: problems and prognosis', *Work, Employment and Society*, 25(1), 51–67.

Duhigg, C. (2014), *The Power of Habit: Why We Do What We Do in Life and Business*, Random House Publishing, New York.

Royle, T. (2001), *Working for McDonald's in Europe: The Unequal Struggle*, Routledge, London.

Wilkinson, A., Townsend, K., Graham, T., and Muurlink, O. (2015), 'Fatal consequences: an analysis of the failed employee voice system at the Bundaberg Hospital', *Asia Pacific Journal of Human Resources*, 53(3), 265–80.

James, J. (2013), 'A new, evidence-based estimate of patient harms associated with hospital care', *Journal of Patient Safety*, 9(3), 122–8.

Kelly, A., and Grant, H. (2019), 'Jailed for a Facebook post: garment workers' rights at risk during Covid-19', *Guardian*, 16 June 2020.

Passa, D. (2019), 'Rugby Australia to terminate Folau deal after anti-gay post', *ABC News*, 11 April 2019.

Chapter 6: Saying goodbye? Downsizing—are human resources assets or liabilities?

Dobbins, T., and Wilkinson, A. (2020), 'Downsizing', in Wilkinson, A., Dundon, T., and Redman, T. (eds), *Contemporary Human Resource Management* (6th edition), Sage, London.

Burrell, G. (1997), *Pandemonium: Towards a Retro-organization Theory*, Sage, London.

Wilkinson, A. (2005), 'Downsizing, rightsizing or dumbsizing? Quality, human resources and the management of sustainability', *Total Quality Management & Business Excellence*, 16(8–9), 1079–88.

ILO (2020), *ILO Monitor 2nd edition: COVID-19 and the World of Work*, ILO, Geneva, April 7.

Frone, M. R., and Blais, A.-R. (2020), 'Organizational downsizing, work conditions, and employee outcomes: identifying targets for workplace intervention among survivors', *International Journal of Environmental Research and Public Health*, 17, 719.

Sahdev, K. (2003), 'Survivors' reactions to downsizing: the importance of contextual factors', *Human Resource Management Journal*, 13(4), 56–74.

Forbes, M. K., and Krueger, R. F. (2019), 'The Great Recession and mental health in the United States', *Clinical Psychological Science*, 7(5), 900–13.

Stebbins, M. (1989), 'Downsizing with "mafia model consultants"', *Business Forum* (Winter), 45–7.

Garfield, A. (1999), 'Barclays shares soar as city welcomes job cuts', *The Independent*, 21 May.

Cascio, W. (1993), 'Downsizing: what do we know, what have we learned?', *Academy of Management Executive*, 7(1), 95–104.

Cascio, W. F., Chatrath, A., and Christie-David, R. A. (2020), 'Antecedents and consequences of employment and asset restructuring', *Academy of Management Journal*, DOI 10.5465/amj.2018.1013.

Budros, A. (1999), 'A conceptual framework for analyzing why organizations downsize', *Organization Science*, 10(1), 69–81.

De Meuse, K., Bergmann, T., and Vanderheiden, P. (1997), 'Corporate downsizing: separating myth from fact', *Journal of Management Inquiry*, 6(2), 168–76.

McCune, J. T., Beatty, R. W., and Montagno, R. V. (1988), 'Downsizing: practices in manufacturing firms', *Human Resource Management*, 27, 145–61, DOI 10.1002/hrm.3930270203.

Hammer, M. (1996), *Beyond Re-engineering*, Harper, New York.

Cole, R. (1993), 'Learning from learning theory: implications for quality improvement of turnover, use of contingent workers, and job rotation policies', *Quality Management Journal*, 1(1), 9–25.

Mellahi, K., and Wilkinson, A. (2010), 'Slash and burn or nip and tuck? Downsizing, innovation and human resources', *International Journal of Human Resource Management*, 21(13), 2291–305.

Young, G. (2015), 'New black sheriff sacks opponents', *Guardian*, 13 May.

Peterson, H. (2015), 'Wal-Mart laid off 2,200 workers, then told them to avoid chocolate and alcohol', *Yahoo Finance*, 1 May, viewed 21 May 2020, <https://finance.yahoo.com/news/wal-mart-laid-off-2-173549197.html>.

Tyler, M., and Wilkinson, A. (2007), 'The tyranny of corporate slenderness: "corporate anorexia" as a metaphor for our age', *Work, Employment and Society*, 21(3), 537–49.

Johnson, B. (2008), 'Electric car manufacturer hit by financial crisis', *Guardian*, 16 October 2008.

Chadwick, C., Hunter, L., and Walston, S. (2004), 'Effects of downsizing practices on the performance of hospitals', *Strategic Management Journal*, 25(5), 405–27.

Brockner, J., Grover, S., Reed, T., DeWitt, R., and O'Malley, M. (1987), 'Survivors' reactions to layoffs: we get by with a little help from our friends', *Administrative Science Quarterly*, 32, 526–42.

Cappelli, P. (2009), 'Alternatives to layoffs', HR Executive Online. Available at: <www.hreonline.com/HRE/story.jsp?storyId=158416635>.

Cameron, K. S., Freeman, S. J., and Mishra, A. K. (1993), 'Downsizing and redesigning organizations', in Huber, G., and Glick, W. (eds), *Organisational Change and Redesign*, Oxford University Press, New York, pp. 19–63.

Cameron, K. S. (1994), 'Strategies for successful organisational downsizing', *Human Resource Management*, 33(2), 189–211.

Welch, J. (2001), *What I've Learned Leading a Great Company and Great People*, Headline Book Publishing, London.

Desai, S. D., Brief, A. P., and George, J. (2009), 'Meaner Managers: A Consequence of Income Inequality', in Kramer, R., Bazerman, M., and Tenbrunsel, A. (eds), *Social Decision Making: Social Dilemmas, Social Values, and Ethical Judgments*, Taylor & Francis, New York, pp. 315–34.

Batt, R. (2018), 'The financial model of the firm, the 'future of work', and employment relations', in Wilkinson, A., Dundon, T., Donaghey, J., and Colvin, A. (eds), *The Routledge Companion to Employment Relations*, Routledge, Abingdon, pp. 467–79.

Tabuchi, H. (2013), illegal-japan-workers-are-sent-to-the-boredom-room, <https://www.nytimes.com/2013/08/17/business/global/layoffs-illegal-japan-workers-are-sent-to-the-boredom-room.html>.

Cascio, W. (2002), 'Strategies for responsible restructuring', *Academy of Management Executive*, 16, 80–91.

Cascio, W. (2014), 'Investing in HR in uncertain times now and in the future', *Advances in Developing Human Resources*, 16(1), 108–22.

McAllister, T. (2001), 'Thomas Cook cuts jobs and pay', *Guardian*, 1 November, viewed 21 May 2020, <https://www.theguardian.com/business/2001/nov/01/travelnews.travel>.

Kaufman, B. E. (2012), 'Wage theory, new deal labor policy, and the great depression: were government and unions to blame?', *ILR Review*, 65(3), 501–32.

Van Wanrooy, B., Bewley, H., Bryson, A., Forth, J., Freeth, S., Stokes, L., and Wood, S. (2013), *Employment Relations in the Shadow of Recession: Findings from the Workplace Employment Relations Study*, Palgrave Macmillan, Basingstoke.

Johnstone, S. (2019), 'Employment practices, labour flexibility and the great recession: an automotive case study', *Economic and Industrial Democracy*, 40(3), 537–59.

Johnstone, S., and Wilkinson, A. (2018), 'The potential of labour–management partnership: a longitudinal case analysis', *British Journal of Management*, 29, 554–70.

Farrell, M., and Mavondo, F. (2004), 'The effect of downsizing strategy and reorientation strategy on a learning orientation', *Personnel Review*, 33(4), 383–402.

Roche, W., and Teague, P. (2012), 'Business partners and working the pumps: human resource managers in the recession', *Human Relations*, 65(10), 1333–58.

Chapter 7: Conclusion

Dobbins, T., Johnstone, S., Kahancová, M., Lamare, R., and Wilkinson, A. (2022), 'Comparative impacts of the COVID-19 crisis on work and employment', *Industrial Relations: A Journal of Economy and Society*.

Collings, D. G., Nyberg, A. J., Wright, P. M., and McMackin, J. (2021), 'Leading through paradox in a COVID-19 world: human resources comes of age', *Human Resource Management Journal*, 2021, 1–15. <https://onlinelibrary.wiley.com/doi/pdf/10.1111/1748-8583.12343>.

Butterick, M., and Charlwood, A. (2021), 'HRM and the COVID-19 pandemic: How can we stop making a bad situation worse?', *Human Resource Management Journal*, 31(4), 847–56.

Winton, A., and Howcroft, D. (2020), 'What COVID-19 tells us about the value of human labour'. http://blog.policy.manchester.ac.uk/posts/2020/04/what-covid-19-tells-us-about-the-value-of-human-labour/.

Wilkinson, A., Barry, M., Gomez, R., and Kaufman, B. E. (2018), 'Taking the pulse at work: an employment relations scorecard for Australia', *Journal of Industrial Relations*, 60(2), 145–75.

Guest, D. (2017), 'Human resource management and employee well-being: towards a new analytic framework', *Human Resource Management Journal*, 27(1), 22–38.

Marchington, M. (2015), 'Human resource management (HRM): too busy looking up to see where it is going longer term?', *Human Resource Management Review*, 25(2), 176–87.

Pfeffer, J. (2018), *Dying for a Paycheck*, Harper Publishing, New York.

Bentley, T. (2019), 'NZ workplace study shows more than quarter of employees feel depressed much of the time', *The Conversation*, 21 August, viewed 10 June, <https://theconversation.com/nz-workplace-study-shows-more-than-quarter-of-employees-feel-depressed-much-of-the-time-118989>.

Ross, S. (2020), 'Commercial laundry discovers it has 25 migrant workers with 31 untapped degrees', *ABC News*, 1 October.

Ghoshal, S. (2005), 'Bad management theories are destroying good management practices', *Academy of Management Learning and Education*, 4(1), 75–91, p. 85.

Fleming, P. (2016), 'How managers came to rule the workplace', *Guardian*, 21 November, viewed 10 June, <https://www.theguardian.com/careers/2016/nov/21/how-managers-came-to-rule-the-workplace>.

Florentine, S. (2016), 'Stop your workers from 'quitting in their seats'',
   CIO, 25 July 2016.
Kochan, T. (2015), *Shaping the Future of Work: What Future Worker,
   Business, Government, and Education Leaders Need to Do for All to
   Prosper*, Business Expert Press, New York.
Ulrich, D., and Yeung, A. (2019), *Reinventing the Organization*,
   Harvard Business Review Press, Boston.

Index

For the benefit of digital users, indexed terms that span two pages (e.g., 52–53) may, on occasion, appear on only one of those pages.

HUMAN RIGHTS
A Very Short Introduction
Andrew Clapham

An appeal to human rights in the face of injustice can be a heartfelt and morally justified demand for some, while for others it remains merely an empty slogan. Taking an international perspective and focusing on highly topical issues such as torture, arbitrary detention, privacy, health and discrimination, this *Very Short Introduction* will help readers to understand for themselves the controversies and complexities behind this vitally relevant issue. Looking at the philosophical justification for rights, the historical origins of human rights and how they are formed in law, Andrew Clapham explains what our human rights actually are, what they might be, and where the human rights movement is heading.

www.oup.com/vsi

INFORMATION
A Very Short Introduction
Luciano Floridi

Luciano Floridi, a philosopher of information, cuts across many subjects, from a brief look at the mathematical roots of information - its definition and measurement in 'bits'- to its role in genetics (we are information), and its social meaning and value. He ends by considering the ethics of information, including issues of ownership, privacy, and accessibility; copyright and open source. For those unfamiliar with its precise meaning and wide applicability as a philosophical concept, 'information' may seem a bland or mundane topic. Those who have studied some science or philosophy or sociology will already be aware of its centrality and richness. But for all readers, whether from the humanities or sciences, Floridi gives a fascinating and inspirational introduction to this most fundamental of ideas.

'Splendidly pellucid.'

Steven Poole, The Guardian

PRIVACY
A Very Short Introduction
Raymond Wacks

Professor Raymond Wacks is a leading international expert on privacy. For more than three decades he has published numerous books and articles on this controversial subject. Privacy is a fundamental value that is under attack from several quarters. Electronic surveillance, biometrics, CCTV, ID cards, RFID codes, online security, the monitoring of employees, the uses and misuses of DNA, - to name but a few - all raise fundamental questions about our right to privacy. This *Very Short Introduction* also analyzes the tension between free speech and privacy generated by intrusive journalism, photography, and gratuitous disclosures by the media of the private lives of celebrities. Professor Wacks concludes this stimulating introduction by considering the future of privacy in our society.

www.oup.com/vsi

Economics
A Very Short Introduction
Partha Dasgupta

Economics has the capacity to offer us deep insights into
some of the most formidable problems of life, and offer
solutions to them too. Combining a global approach with
examples from everyday life, Partha Dasgupta describes the
lives of two children who live very different lives in different
parts of the world: in the Mid-West USA and in Ethiopia. He
compares the obstacles facing them, and the processes that
shape their lives, their families, and their futures. He shows
how economics uncovers these processes, finds explanations
for them, and how it forms policies and solutions.

'An excellent introduction . . . presents mathematical and statistical
findings in straightforward prose.'

Financial Times

ORGANIZATIONS
A Very Short Introduction
Mary Jo Hatch

This *Very Short Introductions* addresses all of these questions and considers many more. Mary Jo Hatch introduces the concept of organizations by presenting definitions and ideas drawn from the a variety of subject areas including the physical sciences, economics, sociology, psychology, anthropology, literature, and the visual and performing arts. Drawing on examples from prehistory and everyday life, from the animal kingdom as well as from business, government, and other formal organizations, Hatch provides a lively and thought provoking introduction to the process of organization.

www.oup.com/vsi